I & II CORINTHIANS

A Devotional Commentary

I & II CORINTHIANS

A Devotional Commentary

Meditations on St. Paul's

First and Second Letters

to the Corinthians

GENERAL EDITOR

Leo Zanchettin

The Word Among Us Press
9639 Doctor Perry Road
Ijamsville, Maryland 21754
www.wordamongus.org
ISBN: 1-59325-002-9

Cover Art:
Raphael
St. Paul preaching at Athens, 1515-16.
Bodycolor on paper mounted onto canvas (tapestry cartoon), 3.4 x 4.4 m.
Victoria & Albert Museum, London/Art Resource, New York

Cover design by Christopher Ranck

Made and printed in the United States of America.

Library of Congress Control Number: 2003105974

Foreword

Love is patient.
Love is kind.
Love is not envious or boastful or arrogant. . . .
Love never fails.
(1 Corinthians 13:4,8)

These very familiar words have been read at countless weddings, and it's no wonder why. What sounds at first like a beautiful poetic description of love is revealed over time to be a set of very challenging statements: Do you want the grace of this wedding day to last a very long time? Then be patient with each other. Do you want to see God's hand in your marriage for years to come? Then make sure you practice kindness. Do you want your marriage to be a sign of God's love and grace to those around you? Then put aside arrogance and envy. This passage tells us that when the storms of life strike—and there's no avoiding them—marriages survive not by romantic feelings alone but by clinging to the Lord and holding fast to his command to love as he loved.

It's no surprise, too, that St. Paul would use these words in a letter to a young church that was struggling with intense storms of its own. The believers in Corinth were so excited about their experiences of the Spirit that they lost sight of the gospel call to love one another as deeply as Jesus loved them. Thinking their extraordinary experiences gave them access to hidden wisdom from God—and consequently made them superior to others—some of the Christians in Corinth began taking advantage of their brothers and sisters. As you might expect, division and mistrust ensued. These were the issues that Paul needed to address.

In every generation, God wants to teach his people anew what it means to be the body of Christ. He wants to reveal to them how to stay close to him and weather the storms that are sure to come, in their church, in their marriage, or in their lives in the world.

There is no better place than in these Corinthian letters to discover the keys to surviving, and even flourishing, as the people of God: Let the Spirit reveal God's wisdom to you (1 Corinthians 2:9-10). Remember that in Christ you hold a priceless treasure, even though you are a "clay jar" (2 Corinthians 4:7). Love and uphold the poor among you (1 Corinthians 11:21-34). Trust that, however weak you may feel, God's grace is more than sufficient (2 Corinthians 12:9-10). And above all else, trust and believe that the love God has for you will never fail (1 Corinthians 13:8).

Paul gave the Corinthians encouragement from the Lord, guidance for difficult times, and a deeper understanding of the truths of the gospel—and these are gifts that we, too, can unwrap. As we do, we'll discover that in our victories as well as in our storms, God is with us, offering us his love, his power, and his mercy.

We want to thank everyone who has made this commentary possible. Many of the meditations produced here were initially developed for *The Word Among Us* monthly publication, and we want to thank all of the writers of these meditations for granting us permission to reprint their work. We also want to thank Fr. Joseph Wimmer, O.S.A., Fr. Carlo Notaro, Hallie Riedel, Bob French, Theresa Leyva, Jeanne Kun, and Louise Perrotta for contributing the longer chapters. And finally, many thanks go to Kathy Mayne for her tireless administrative work in gathering all the material that went into this book. May the Lord abundantly bless them all.

Leo Zanchettin
General Editor

Table of Contents

Letters of Wisdom, Passion, and Guidance

An Introduction to First and Second Corinthians

by Fr. Joseph F. Wimmer, O.S.A.

One of the most important destinations of St. Paul's missionary journeys was Corinth, a port city in the southwestern region of Greece known as Achaia. It lies about sixty miles directly west of Athens. The ancient Greek city-state of Corinth was destroyed by a Roman general in 146 B.C., but was rebuilt by Julius Caesar in 44 B.C. as a haven for freedmen—both Jews and Gentiles—from Greece, Egypt, Palestine, and Syria. Corinth soon became the capital of the province of Achaia and was governed by a Roman proconsul. During Paul's first visit there, the proconsul's name was Gallio, whose administration in Corinth can be dated to about A.D. 51-52. According to Acts 18:11, Paul's first apostolic ministry in Corinth lasted eighteen months, during which time he brought many converts to the Christian faith. After moving on, he remained in contact with them primarily by letter. We are told of only one further visit of Paul to the Corinthians; it was a painful one, though he had planned to see them again after that (2 Corinthians 12:14; 13:2).

The so-called "first" letter to the Corinthians was not really the first time Paul had written to them. In 1 Corinthians 5:9 he speaks of a previous letter, but unfortunately it has been lost to us. Nor is Second Corinthians his second letter to them, for in it he discusses a "severe letter" he had written them (2 Corinthians 2:3-4; 7:8-9), which too seems to have been lost, though some commentators believe it is preserved as 2 Corinthians 10-13.

Paul follows the general style of Hellenistic letters, with his name first; sometimes augmented by a coworker or two; then the name of the addressee; a greeting, which for him was often "grace and peace"; a short note of thanksgiving; and finally the body of the letter. Letters were usually dictated, and the sender of the letter sometimes signed it personally, as Paul did in 1 Corinthians 16:21.

First Corinthians

First Corinthians was occasioned by a series of questions posed by the Corinthian community to Paul in a letter (7:1) which was probably delivered by Stephanas, Fortunatus, and Achaicus (16:17). Paul was living in Ephesus at the time and wrote the letter probably in the spring of A.D. 56 or 57 (16:8). His answers to their questions contain rich material and make this one of the longest of Paul's letters. While treating such concrete matters as the need for church unity, proper sexual morality, dignified Eucharistic celebrations, correct attitudes toward civil courts, and how to deal with food offered to idols, Paul set these topics in the profound theological context of divine wisdom, humility, love, the power of Christ's resurrection, and a majestic vision of eternal life.

Introduction (1 Corinthians 1:1-9). Paul begins by emphasizing his authority as an apostle called by Christ himself. The Corinthians too have been consecrated by Christ and are thought of as the special people of God. Paul thanks God because they have been blessed by his divine gifts so as to attain salvation at the Second Coming of Christ. Paul's instructions are meant to guide them safely to that day of final judgment.

Divisions in the Church (1 Corinthians 1:10–4:21). Paul now turns to the first major problem confronting him in the Corinthian community: the existence of religious factions. Some were claiming a special connection to Paul, while others said they belonged to Apollos, Cephas, or Christ. Apollos was a convert from Judaism in Alexandria, Egypt, and was a very successful preacher in the early Christian church. He ministered at Ephesus and later at Corinth (Acts 18:24—19:1). At the time of the writing of this letter, Apollos seems to have been living again at Ephesus, along with Paul (1 Corinthians 16:12). We have every reason to believe that they were coworkers and friends (3:5-9; 4:6). Cephas is the Aramaic name for Peter (both mean "rock"). He too may have preached in Corinth—Paul mentions his missionary activity in 9:5—or he may simply have represented a more conservative form of the faith to Corinthian Christians of Jewish background. The "Christ" faction may have been a special group of charismatics who emphasized their mystical union with Jesus to the exclusion of their membership in the larger Christian community. Paul urges all these groups to form one community, united in the same Christ who was crucified for them all.

Improper Conduct (1 Corinthians 5–6). News had reached Paul that a member of the Corinthian church was living in marriage with his stepmother—a situation that was contrary to Scripture (Leviticus 18:8) and also forbidden by the Council of Jerusalem in A.D. 49 (Acts 15:20). Paul demands a stop to this practice, along with sexual immorality in general. He also criticized their use of pagan civil courts to settle disputes among members of the community.

Marriage and Virginity (1 Corinthians 7). Within marriage both husband and wife have equal rights to each other's body and are to remain faithful to one another. But if an "unbelieving" husband or wife separates, they are allowed to do so, and the partner is no longer bound (7:15). This is the basis of the "Pauline privilege" in later Catholic legislation. Virginity is treated by Paul in an eschatological context; that is, the world as we know it is passing away quickly (7:31). A virginal life dedicated to God is concerned primarily about the relationship with God and is not divided in spirit (7:32-35). Yet Paul is careful to state that those who marry do not sin (7:28).

Offerings to Idols (1 Corinthians 8–10). The seemingly outdated debate about eating food offered to idols rests on some important basic principles. Although idols are merely statues of supposed gods who do not really exist, food offered to them in pagan sacrifice is not really sanctified and may be eaten by anyone. Yet some might be weak in their faith and even scandalized at this practice. While insisting on its legitimacy, Paul is determined never to eat meat again if it causes others to sin (8:13). In everything we do, we are to do it for the glory of God (10:31).

Liturgical Assemblies (1 Corinthians 11). Chapter eleven begins with Paul stating his desire that the women of Corinth wear veils during public worship, while the men are to have their heads uncovered. Apparently this was a source of tension because of cultural differences among the Corinthians. Paul wanted them to follow the Palestinian custom of women veiled in public, though this custom was not generally held in Greece. A second issue was abusive behavior during the meal that preceded the Eucharist. On this occasion, Paul cited the basic tradition about the Last Supper in order to encourage reverence and faith. Those who eat the consecrated bread and wine unworthily are guilty of "profaning the body and blood of the Lord" (11:27).

Gifts of the Spirit (1 Corinthians 12–14). Although individuals receive different gifts from the Holy Spirit, they are members of one body and should utilize these gifts for the good of the whole community. And all these gifts are dependent upon the greatest of gifts, love (1 Corinthians 13). At charismatic meetings one is allowed to speak in tongues, though Paul would rather speak five words of instruction than ten thousand in tongues (14:19).

The Resurrection (1 Corinthians 15). Christ truly rose from the dead, not only for himself but also for us, as the "first fruits" of those who have died (15:20). We too will rise on the last day, for first fruits refer to that part of the harvest which was given to God in order to sanctify the rest. Paul then speculates on the nature of our resurrected "spiritual body" (15:44). This is given to us by Christ who is called a "life-giving Spirit" (15:45). The identity of Christ with the Spirit probably means Christ as spiritually present and active after his resurrection. Paul then urges us to be faithful to the end, assured that our efforts will not be in vain (15:58).

Closing Remarks (1 Corinthians 16). After giving some final directions about a collection in Corinth for the church of Jerusalem, Paul briefly sums up his travel plans and sends greetings to the whole community, with special mention of certain people. He ends with a note in his own hand, urging love for the Lord who is to come soon: "*Marana tha*" (16:22).

Second Corinthians

This letter is generally dated to the autumn of A.D. 56 or 57, about six months after First Corinthians. It was written by Paul primarily as a self-defense against accusations that he was unreliable. He had twice changed the date of a proposed visit to the Corinthian community and learned that certain Jewish Christian preachers had come among them disputing some of his teachings. He felt the need to write them a strong letter and also to regulate a collection that he was taking up among them for the Christian community in Jerusalem. Although these were difficult circumstances for both Paul and the Corinthians, we learn much about Paul's missionary work and spirituality. This is his most personal letter and is very revealing about Paul the man.

Introduction and the New Covenant (2 Corinthians 1–3). Paul gives his name and title as apostle, adds Timothy's name as well, and addresses the community to whom he was writing, "the church of God in Corinth." In the customary thanksgiving section which follows, Paul thanks God for consoling him in his grievous afflictions, which were so great that he feared he might die. He explains his reasons for not visiting the Corinthians as planned and assures them he is still trustworthy. In contrast to Moses, who put a veil over his face, Paul is a bold minister of the new covenant, a minister of the life-giving Spirit (3:6). Later he explains that the Lord is the Spirit who brings freedom (3:17). This identification of the Lord with the Spirit is very deep, but it may well refer to the risen Christ as spiritually present and active. We are gradually being transformed into the likeness of Christ through faith and in the power of his Spirit (3:18).

Paul as Minister (2 Corinthians 4–7). Paul shows that he is a reliable minister of Christ because he preaches not himself but Jesus Christ as Lord (4:5). This glorious message, this treasure, is held in "earthen vessels," that is, fragile human beings (4:7). Paul then speaks of his afflictions, but always with a note of hope: beaten down but not destroyed, worried but not in despair, willing to die for the sake of Christ (4:8-11). Paul longed to enter eternal life. He expresses this in the imagery of being clothed. Over the clothing of the grace of our present life he hopes to be clothed with glory. While in the body, we are in exile from our true home, heaven. Paul wants to please God at all times, aware that at the judgment seat of Christ he will be judged according to his deeds (5:1-10). And yet, even now, transformation through grace by being united to Christ in the new covenant amounts to a "new creation" (5:17).

The Collection for Jerusalem (2 Corinthians 8–9). At the heart of Paul's ministry was a desire to bring all the Christian communities together as one church, the church of God that is gathered here or there. There was a split line between Jewish and Greek Christian communities, and since the mother church in Jerusalem was particularly poor, Paul felt that a collection taken up in the Hellenistic churches for their fellow Christians in Jerusalem would bring a greater unity to them all. It would be the image of the "one body" of 1 Corinthians 12 acted out in a concrete way. Within his plea for generosity, Paul writes a profound text of Christology, the example of Jesus, who though "rich" in eternity prior to his birth "became poor" for our sakes so that through his poverty we might become rich (8:9).

Self-Defense (2 Corinthians 10–13). The letter concludes with a passionate openness of heart toward the Corinthian community. Paul felt that he had been misrepresented to them by other preachers and wanted to set the record straight. Accused of being weak, feeble, and of no account, he courageously—"foolishly"—wrote to them of his mystical visions and pastoral toughness. He endured all manner of hardships and dangers in his ministry: shipwrecks, beatings, stonings, imprisonments, and more. Yet, during all this time, his one concern was the welfare of the people to whom he was bringing the good news of salvation, his "anxiety for all the churches" (11:28). With a spirit of faith and great love he ends the letter with a blessing we still repeat today: "The grace of the Lord Jesus Christ and the love of God and the fellowship of the Holy Spirit be with you all" (13:14).

Letters for All of Us

There's something universally intriguing about Paul's relationship with the Christians in Corinth. Perhaps it's the city's reputation for immorality. Or maybe it's the fact that both letters give us poignant pictures of Paul at his most personal and vulnerable. Or maybe it's because Paul's troubled relationship with this community feels the most "human" to us and speaks to us in times of tension or uncertainty in our relationships. The meditations that make up this book are meant to help us mine the riches of wisdom—both human and divine—that God revealed through Paul's relationship with the believers in Corinth.

As we pray through these letters, we shouldn't be surprised to find various aspects of our own lives and of the church of our age reflected in them. After all, much of what the Spirit said two thousand years ago through Paul is just as applicable to us today. This is the wonder of all Scripture: Through it, God continues to reach out and offer us his wisdom, correction, love, and compassion. Even when we feel as confused, as misled, and even as stubborn as the Corinthians, God is with us, ready to pour out all the grace we need to stay close to him.

A Closer Look at Paul's Corinth

by Bob French

Imagine that you go up to your attic and find an old photograph album you've never seen before. You take it out, dust it off, and peer at faded pictures of people long dead, wondering who they were. Now think of those people as the Corinthians, some of the very first Christians, who are your brothers and sisters in Christ. "Where did they come from?" you might wonder. "What was their life like, and how did they relate to the world around them?" Chances are, the more we know about these people, these ancient ancestors in the faith, the more we'll find we have in common with them—and the more Paul's letters to them will speak to us. With this in mind, let's take an in-depth look at the city of Corinth and the Christians who lived there, as well as the customs and attitudes of the culture of which they were a part.

Crossroads of Culture, Wealth, and Pleasure. From what historians tell us, we can highlight three hallmarks of Corinthian culture in the first century: its cosmopolitan character, its wealth, and its love of pleasure. In Paul's time, Corinth was a crossroads of the ancient world. Located just a few miles from the Isthmus of Corinth, it controlled the land routes between southern and central Greece. It was also a nexus for trade between the eastern and western Mediterranean and points beyond.

Since there was then no canal cut through the Isthmus, Corinth was in control of the eastern and western harbors that separated the Saronic Gulf, on the eastern side, from the Gulf of Corinth to the west. Very soon after its colonization, Corinth became known as a major commercial center. A constant traffic of goods flowed in and out of the city from all over the known world, and merchants sold these goods in the city's huge marketplace (*agora*).

Corinth boasted not only a diversity of goods but of religions as well. On a high hill overlooking the city—the Acrocorinth—sat the temple of Aphrodite. But temples could be found throughout Corinth honoring numerous Greek, Roman, and even Egyptian, gods. It's also widely assumed that since many Jews lived in Corinth, the city probably had a synagogue. Needless to say, the people of Corinth represented many different cultures. Corinth was founded by the Greeks, conquered and colonized by the Romans, and populated with both, as well as with Jews, Phoenicians, Anatolians, and others. At its peak, Corinth was probably home to about eighty to one hundred thousand people, a very large city by ancient standards.

All of these factors contributed to Corinth's great wealth. It was largely the city's services to visiting merchants, tourists, and travelers that generated the greatest amount of income. However, most of the people, including most of the Christians in Corinth, lived somewhere in the middle of the economic ladder: neither very wealthy, as the most powerful Roman citizens were, nor very poor.

Being so open to the world and so prosperous, it was to be expected that the Corinthians loved a good time. As one historian noted, visitors regarded their stay in the city as a participation in an ongoing festival. Various celebrations honored the gods, often accompanied by lavish banquets. Corinth also boasted a fifteen-thousand-seat theater, and had the honor of hosting the nearby Isthmian games. These games, which took place every two years, were rivaled only by the Olympics in popularity. They were so popular, in fact, that they were advertised on Corinthian coins. It was probably these games that Paul speaks of in 1 Corinthians 9:24-27, when he tells his readers to compete for an incorruptible crown instead of a corruptible one: Winners at the Isthmian games were rewarded with a crown of withered celery.

Unfortunately, as Paul must have known, some of the pleasures the Corinthians enjoyed were less than wholesome. The legend that the temple of Aphrodite was once the base for one thousand temple prostitutes is probably untrue, but there was definitely prostitution in the city, as this ancient saying attests: "Not for every man is the voyage to Corinth." Similarly, the verb *korinthiazo* ("to act like a Corinthian") came to be a synonym for sexual license.

One commentator probably summarized Corinth's culture best when he asserted that Corinth resembled a combination of New York, Los Angeles, and Las Vegas.

Early Church Organization. Given this cosmopolitan, eclectic, even hurly-burly environment, we might well wonder how the Christians in Corinth could ever maintain their faith and their unity as brothers and sisters in Christ. One way was to meet regularly in the homes of the wealthier members. Scholars surmise that they structured their groups after the pattern of different organizations prevalent at the time, whose influence can still be seen in the structure of the modern church.

These organizations included the household, or *oikos*, and the collegium, or Roman voluntary association. The *oikos* had a household structure in which the male head, or *paterfamilias*, wielded authority over all the members of his household—his wife, children, blood relatives, slaves, and livestock. While the early Christians maintained lines of authority in their groups, they were much more democratic than traditional households. The *collegium* was another structure, this time based on a patron-client relationship, with the patron often providing financial support for the group. The early Christian groups had wealthy patrons as well, but they were not necessarily the leaders. Collegium membership was usually by choice, and ritual and social activities were important.

The Corinthians may have also drawn from the organizational structure of the typical synagogue, which stressed the Jews' identity as the people of God and emphasized their need to separate from the world. It's also possible that they found some inspiration from the philosophical schools in the city, in which teaching and exhorting were the principal elements—an emphasis to which the Christians added the phenomena of speaking in tongues and prophesying (1 Corinthians 14).

Factions and Divisions. Unfortunately, the very groups that provided support for the church could also generate conflict—especially when worldly concerns like status, wealth, and authority became too strong. Recent research has indicated strongly that such issues may well have played a major role in several of the conflicts Paul addresses in his letters. However, it is important to see that in the ancient world, wealth did not automatically ensure status or authority. For example, a Roman citizen who had little money could have been treated with more respect than a wealthy noncitizen. (See, for instance, the way Paul was treated in Acts 22:23-29.)

The very factions Paul mentions in 1 Corinthians 1–4 may have been the result of exaggerated loyalty to one head of a household church who had higher status with the group because he or she was a better orator than Paul, or simply because he had established an aura of authority by baptizing other members of the group.

The division that came about over the Lord's Supper that Paul addresses in 1 Corinthians 11:17-33 was another conflict that may have arisen due to issues of status. Paul complains that when people come together for the Lord's Supper, they are humiliating those who "have nothing." A recent line of inquiry has focused on the possible social divisions that could have caused this problem.

The suggestion is that some of the Corinthian households would have a private meal before the Lord's Supper, and give the better food to the wealthier members of the congregation who had provided more for the community. Then, those who came later—usually the poorer members of the group—brought little food and so stayed hungry.

Although, as Paul says, not many of the Corinthians were influential or noble-born (1 Corinthians 1:26), at least some were. Crispus, whom Paul baptized, was the leader of worship at a synagogue, which meant that he probably contributed funds to its construction. Similarly, other believers, such as Gaius, Stephanas, and Chloe, had their own houses and were able to host fellow Christians.

The factor of wealth and status could also help to explain Paul's comment about meat offered to idols. His initial concern seems not to have been that some Christians were actually eating sacrificed meat—since he held that the pagan gods did not really exist—but the fact that those who did eat it could influence those with weak consciences who thought eating the meat was wrong. In any case, it is certainly true that in the first century, the rich were more likely to be able to eat meat.

Those who were wealthy could also have been the ones Paul complains about in 1 Corinthians 6, who were engaging in lawsuits against fellow church members. It is true that litigation was quite common in the Greco-Roman world, but it was often the case that the rich brought suit against their poorer neighbors.

A different kind of status may well have been at issue in Paul's writings about the charismatic gifts, where he downplays the gift of tongues because it was being used in an inconsiderate and disorderly fashion (1 Corinthians 14). It is clear that Paul is talking to those in the congregation who were "puffed up" because they spoke in tongues. These people may have seen tongues as an indication of spiritual superiority—a sign that they belonged to a higher status group. If so, it was because they held onto contemporary philosophies that devalued the body and placed too great an emphasis on spiritual experiences.

Status of Women. It is certainly true that wherever he established churches, Paul allowed women a great deal of freedom. Commentators note that in Corinth itself, Paul names Chloe as the head of a household (1 Corinthians 1:11). Likewise, he calls Phoebe, who lived in Cenchrae, the eastern harbor of Corinth, a *diakonos* or minister (Romans 16:1), and he names Junias an apostle (16:7). All this would seem to go along with a trend toward greater freedom for women that began to be seen in the Roman Empire about that time. As one researcher into ancient families found, some first-century women owned houses, others were patrons of cults, and some even practiced law. While these were mostly women of the upper class, even in the lower classes women had a lot of mobility.

Paul's views on the role of women were certainly more liberated than the ideas of his contemporaries, and would help to explain why they were allowed to be leaders in his congregations. However, Paul was not just a "free spirit" who liked to experiment. Most scholars agree that he held to a hierarchical view of male/female relationships ("The head of the woman is the man"; "Woman is the reflection of man's glory"—1 Corinthians 11:3,7). Nevertheless, his concept of authority was very different from the Greco-Roman idea of hierarchy, in which being the head meant complete domination. In Paul's view, it is the Lord who orders everything, so there is no room for prideful attitudes: "In the Lord, however, woman is not independent of man, nor is man independent of woman" (11:11).

Conclusion. Admittedly, our picture of the Corinthians is still a bit fuzzy. Some things we will never know, and some things will be debated for years to come. But it's clear that the Corinthians had more in common with us than we might think at first glance. Their city was in some ways a microcosm of our own society. Corinth was a multicultural and diverse place. Most of its people had a fair degree of prosperity. And there were many voices in Corinth that competed with the gospel for their attention. Their choices were not always easy, and sometimes following the Lord meant going against everything their culture told them was acceptable. Even in their own community, there were those who argued about how things should be done. But thankfully, we, like the Corinthians, have Paul's most enduring advice on how to handle any problem: "So faith, hope, love abide, these three; but the greatest of these is love" (1 Corinthians 13:13).

Wisdom and Folly

1 CORINTHIANS 1–4

1 Corinthians 1:1-9

[1] Paul, called by the will of God to be an apostle of Christ Jesus, and our brother Sos'thenes,
[2] To the church of God which is at Corinth, to those sanctified in Christ Jesus, called to be saints together with all those who in every place call on the name of our Lord Jesus Christ, both their Lord and ours:
[3] Grace to you and peace from God our Father and the Lord Jesus Christ.
[4] I give thanks to God always for you because of the grace of God which was given you in Christ Jesus, [5] that in every way you were enriched in him with all speech and all knowledge — [6] even as the testimony to Christ was confirmed among you — [7] so that you are not lacking in any spiritual gift, as you wait for the revealing of our Lord Jesus Christ; [8] who will sustain you to the end, guiltless in the day of our Lord Jesus Christ. [9] God is faithful, by whom you were called into the fellowship of his Son, Jesus Christ our Lord.

[He] will sustain you to the end. (1 Corinthians 1:8)

Corinth was an important port city in the Roman Empire, and as such it was a popular meeting place of many different cultures—not all of them wholesome! Sexual immorality was rampant, and the many shady business deals struck in Corinth kept the legal profession busy with countless lawsuits. It's no wonder, then, that the church in Corinth would be affected by similar problems, some of which threatened its very life. What a difficult set of problems Paul had to deal with as he sought to counsel this Christian community!

Yet, despite all the issues that Paul had to deal with—and despite some of the hurtful things the Corinthians said about him—Paul remained optimistic. Why? Was he out of touch? Overly idealistic? Just plain naïve? Not at all. Paul knew the forces arrayed against the church, and he felt deeply the arrows directed against him. But he also knew from years of experience how faithful to his promises God is. He knew that, whatever happened in this struggling, divided community, God would prevail. The blood of Christ had sealed an eternal covenant with them—and with all Christians.

Do you believe that when you give your life to Jesus, he accepts it and keeps it close to his heart? Do you believe that when you consecrate your children to Jesus, he takes them to his heart? You may be surrounded by problems and difficulties from without, and even from within. Things may not make much sense right now. But it's not unrealistic to keep trusting and hoping and even rejoicing in the outworking of God's plans. It's not naïve or idealistic to do so. It's realistic. God is faithful, and he will help us overcome all obstacles.

There are times when it may cost you everything to keep trusting and relying on God's promises. The problems may seem insurmountable. But that's where the grace is. It's when we continue to surrender ourselves and our circumstances to the Lord that we begin to know his presence, his consolation, and the unfolding of his plans in ways we would never have imagined. May we never let our circumstances rob us of our joy and hope in the Lord!

"Lord Jesus, I commit my life and my circumstances to you. I trust in your bountiful love and your covenant with your people and with me."

1 Corinthians 1:10-17

[10] I appeal to you, brethren, by the name of our Lord Jesus Christ, that all of you agree and that there be no dissensions among you, but that you be united in the same mind and the same judgment. [11] For it has been reported to me by Chlo'e's people that there is quarreling among you, my brethren. [12] What I mean is that each one of you says, "I belong to Paul," or "I belong to Apol'los," or "I belong to Cephas," or "I belong to Christ." [13] Is Christ divided? Was Paul crucified for you? Or were you baptized in the name of Paul? [14] I am thankful that I baptized none of you except Crispus and Ga'ius; [15] lest any one should say that you were baptized in my name. [16] (I did baptize also the household of Steph'anas. Beyond that, I do not know whether I baptized any one else.) [17] For Christ did not send me to baptize but to preach the gospel, and not with eloquent wisdom, lest the cross of Christ be emptied of its power.

During his second missionary journey, Paul spent close to two years in Corinth—one of the largest commerce centers in the Roman Empire—working to establish a Christian community there (Acts 18:1-18). Many people in Corinth embraced his message of salvation through Jesus Christ and became believers. The Corinthian Christians were richly blessed by God, especially in the area of spiritual gifts (1 Corinthians 1:4-7). Yet in spite of these great blessings from the Lord, the fledgling church was troubled by quarrels and internal rivalries (1:11-12).

As different factions developed, the Corinthians were in danger of losing the unity that is essential to the body of Christ.

Concerned, Paul appealed to them to end their bickering and seek after unity (1 Corinthians 1:10). Lest the Corinthians lose sight of Jesus, Paul also reminded them that the Christian faith they had embraced, as well as their experience of being a community filled with God's blessings, rested on Jesus Christ and the power of his cross. It didn't depend primarily on the special talents of Christian leaders like himself or Apollos or Cephas (1:13,17).

Keeping our eyes fixed on Jesus and his cross is a necessary safeguard for us, too. In a world that idolizes celebrities and exalts popular personalities, Christians stand as a people rooted in God first and people second. It's only through the cross that the heavens are opened, our sins are forgiven, and we are filled with the Holy Spirit. At its very core, this is the church.

The next time you go to Mass, unite yourself with the words of the Eucharistic Prayer, especially the prayer for the church: "Watch over it, Lord, and guide it; grant it peace and unity throughout the world. . . . We pray to you, our living and true God, for our well-being and redemption." Let the Spirit show you what a glorious thing it is to be joined to all your brothers and sisters in the body of Christ by Jesus himself. As you pray, may Christ increase your love for every member of his church!

"Spirit of God, blow afresh on every member of the body of Christ today. Open our eyes to the great inheritance that is ours in Christ and in the church."

1 Corinthians 1:18-25

[18] For the word of the cross is folly to those who are perishing, but to us who are being saved it is the power of God. [19] For it is written,

"I will destroy the wisdom of the wise,
and the cleverness of the clever I will thwart."

[20] Where is the wise man? Where is the scribe? Where is the debater of this age? Has not God made foolish the wisdom of the world? [21] For since, in the wisdom of God, the world did not know God through wisdom, it pleased God through the folly of what we preach to save those who believe. [22] For Jews demand signs and Greeks seek wisdom, [23] but we preach Christ crucified, a stumbling block to Jews and folly to Gentiles, [24] but to those who are called, both Jews and Greeks, Christ the power of God and the wisdom of God. [25] For the foolishness of God is wiser than men, and the weakness of God is stronger than men.

By its very nature, God's wisdom tends to humble our limited human wisdom. Through the wisdom of the cross, we have all been rescued from the inevitability of eternal death and are now offered eternal life. This was the central truth that Paul sought to teach the Corinthian church (1 Corinthians 1:21).

The sight of Jesus on the cross demolishes our trust in our cleverness and our abilities. It shows up our inability to figure God out and proves instead that we are in need of a love far greater and far more different than any kind of love we could ever imagine on our own.

To many people, a crucified savior seems absurd. They reject the idea that humans are unable to achieve lasting peace and justice apart from the grace of God. Some people spend a lifetime seeking and accumulating human wisdom and yet never grasp the wisdom of the cross—or the salvation that it brings.

"Let no one deceive himself," Paul told the Corinthians. "If any one among you thinks that he is wise in this age, let him become a fool . . . . For the wisdom of this world is folly with God" (1 Corinthians 3:18-19). Brought face to face with God's wisdom manifested in the cross, we have the opportunity to recognize our folly and so take a step toward true wisdom.

Godly wisdom is a gift of the spirit. It is the oil that the foolish virgins lacked (Matthew 25:1-13), something that no one but God himself can give. Have you opened your heart to this divine wisdom? Are you willing to let the wisdom of the cross touch your life? Have you come to know the love of Christ crucified? Can you let the cross pry you loose from relying on your own wisdom and strength? Let us all keep pressing on to know Christ more intimately and deeply.

"Father, the wisest thing I can do is admit my foolishness and need for your wisdom. Let the oil of the Spirit burn brightly in me. Let it replace the darkness of my self-reliance and sin. Let the wisdom of Jesus' cross reshape my life."

1 Corinthians 1:26-31

[26] For consider your call, brethren; not many of you were wise according to worldly standards, not many were powerful, not many were of noble birth; [27] but God chose what is foolish in the world to shame the wise, God chose what is weak in the world to shame the strong, [28] God chose what is low and despised in the world, even things that are not, to bring to nothing things that are, [29] so that no human being might boast in the presence of God. [30] He is the source of your life in Christ Jesus, whom God made our wisdom, our righteousness and sanctification and redemption; [31] therefore, as it is written, "Let him who boasts, boast of the Lord."

St. Paul often spoke of "boasting," not in ourselves but in the Lord (1 Corinthians 1:31; 2 Corinthians 10:17; Galatians 6:14; Ephesians 2:9; Philippians 3:3). As he understood it, boasting didn't mean bragging about our accomplishments as much as it meant glorifying the source of these accomplishments. In Paul's view, we can boast about our accomplishments only as we acknowledge that God is the source of the good things in our lives (1 Corinthians 1:30). We "boast in the Lord" most perfectly not when we brag about Jesus, but when we place our trust and confidence in him and in his power to meet all our needs.

Jesus' parable of the talents (Matthew 25:14-30) is an excellent illustration of this truth. In the parable, Jesus points out the different ways in which people approach God's gifts. The good stewards relied heavily upon ("boasted in") what the master had given them, and as a result they received a full return on their investment. The lazy steward, on the other hand, could not see the value of his master's gift. He did not consider it strong enough or reliable enough to invest in and base his life upon. To him, it was good only as a buried-away last resort. Because he didn't see its value, he lost it altogether.

How about you? Do you rely on the grace of God? Do you see it as a priceless treasure? Are you sufficiently confident in his grace that you base your life upon it and make decisions according to how trustworthy the Lord is? Do you trust that in God's hands you have nothing to fear? The more we invest in the love and grace that God has poured into our lives, the more powerfully we will see him working in us and through us.

God is worthy of our confidence. Every day he showers us with grace and he asks us to invest in this grace to the point that we rely on it for the strength and wisdom we need to live. This is what it means to boast in the Lord, and no one who boasts in God will ever be put to shame.

"Heavenly Father, I know that every good thing I have comes from you. I praise you for redeeming me and filling me with your grace. May I always rely on you alone."

1 Corinthians 2:1-5

[1] When I came to you, brethren, I did not come proclaiming to you the testimony of God in lofty words or wisdom. [2] For I decided to know nothing among you except Jesus Christ and him crucified. [3] And I was with you in weakness and in much fear and trembling; [4] and my speech and my message were not in plausible words of wisdom, but in demonstration of the Spirit and of power, [5] that your faith might not rest in the wisdom of men but in the power of God.

How we love to complicate matters—to work out grand strategies and "wise" reasons for the things that we do. This is especially true when it comes to our faith life. Many people shy away from something as powerful as prayer because they find it too simplistic. They either think that God won't hear them or they rely so much on their own wisdom that they miss the opportunity for God to work powerfully in their lives. St. John Chrysostom, one of the early Fathers of the Church, explained Paul's logic in this way: "In these words, 'I am crucified with Christ,' Paul alludes to baptism. . . . For as by death he signifies not what is commonly understood, but a death to sin; so by life, he signifies a deliverance from sin. For a man cannot live to God other than by dying to sin."

The Corinthians were working "overtime" in their efforts to figure out which of the disciples they would follow. They were also working hard to establish good reasons for allowing immoral behavior. But Paul saw through their "wisdom" and reminded them of the first time he spoke to them: "not in . . . wisdom, but in demonstration of the Spirit and of power" (1 Corinthians 2:4).

How like the Corinthians we can be! How often do we use our own wisdom, unaided by the Spirit, to create strategies that we hope will perfect our faith. Yet, it is the power of God in our lives that is the bedrock of our faith. God knows how vital it is that we experience Jesus in a life-changing way. It is crucial that we know in our heart of hearts that he is alive, that he loves us, and that he wants to speak to us. In reality, it's the Spirit who is working overtime, urging us to turn to Jesus in faith, to obey his word, and to love God and each other. We don't have to devise our own independent plans—the Holy Spirit will lead us.

Let us open our hearts to the Spirit so that he can heal us, protect us from sin, and direct our lives. As he pours grace and healing into our hearts, a beautiful cycle of faithfulness and blessing will occur. Jesus promised that he will never forsake us; we can trust him to keep his word. Each day offers us an opportunity to receive the power of God in our lives. Let's set aside our own "wisdom" and open our hearts to God.

"Holy Spirit, help me to be open to your plan for my life and to forsake my tendencies to use my own wisdom. I repent of the sin that hinders your work in my heart. Transform me and reveal your greatness."

1 Corinthians 2:6-16

[6] Yet among the mature we do impart wisdom, although it is not a wisdom of this age or of the rulers of this age, who are doomed to pass away. [7] But we impart a secret and hidden wisdom of God, which God decreed before the ages for our glorification. [8] None of the rulers of this age understood this; for if they had, they would not have crucified the Lord of glory. [9] But, as it is written,

"What no eye has seen, nor ear heard,
nor the heart of man conceived,
what God has prepared for those who love him,"

[10] God has revealed to us through the Spirit. For the Spirit searches everything, even the depths of God. [11] For what person knows a man's thoughts except the spirit of the man which is in him? So also no one comprehends the thoughts of God except the Spirit of God. [12] Now we have received not the spirit of the world, but the Spirit which is from God, that we might understand the gifts bestowed on us by God. [13] And we impart this in words not taught by human

wisdom but taught by the Spirit, interpreting spiritual truths to those who possess the Spirit.
[14] The unspiritual man does not receive the gifts of the Spirit of God, for they are folly to him, and he is not able to understand them because they are spiritually discerned. [15] The spiritual man judges all things, but is himself to be judged by no one. [16] "For who has known the mind of the Lord so as to instruct him?" But we have the mind of Christ.

Imagine that through a relief organization, you have begun to sponsor a young woman in Ethiopia, and you and she have become pen pals. Her most recent letter to you is filled with stories about life in her village, and she tells you how grateful she is for your help. But she has one question: "In your last letter, you told me about an ice cream party you gave for your youngest child. Please, what is this ice cream? Is it a kind of food? What does it taste like?"

How would you answer? How could you possibly describe the taste of ice cream to a person who has never had any? How would you give her a sense of how it feels in the mouth, and how it tastes on the tongue, when she has never even seen it?

This is one way we can understand Paul's words about the "secret and hidden" wisdom of God, which he says can now be revealed to us "through the Spirit" (1 Corinthians 2:7,10). Paul understood that it's one thing to have an intellectual grasp of the truths about God's love, mercy, and power, but it's another thing altogether to experience this love, mercy, and power in our lives. It's like the difference between a theoretical understanding of ice cream and the experience of actually tasting it for the first time.

Paul saw that some of the Christians in Corinth were drifting away from his message of a crucified Messiah and were becoming enamored of rival philosophies. While these new philosophies may have intrigued the Corinthians' minds, Paul knew that these philosophies were incapable of feeding their hearts. And that made all the difference between a close-knit community of believers and a fragmented group prone to pride, division, and scandal. Paul understood that only the Holy Spirit could rebuild and protect the unity that was being eroded in Corinth. And this would only happen as the people spent time in prayer, asking the Spirit to reveal Jesus to them more and more.

God has an unending supply of grace and wisdom to pour out upon us. He even created us with the capacity to hear from his Spirit. Why? Because without this revelation, our life of faith is incomplete and vulnerable. God wants to make the truths that we know in our minds come alive in our hearts so that we can experience his vitality and refreshment every day, in times of difficulty and trial as well as in times of unity and peace. The gospel is not just one among many philosophies of life. It is life itself! And we can know this life as we open our hearts and ask his Spirit to reveal this life to us.

"Holy Spirit, come and fill me with your truth. Transform my times of prayer and Scripture reading into intimate encounters with Jesus, who is the way, the truth, and the life. By your grace, may I taste your love, not just understand it."

1 Corinthians 3:1-9

[1] But I, brethren, could not address you as spiritual men, but as men of the flesh, as babes in Christ. [2] I fed you with milk, not solid food; for you were not ready for it; and even yet you are not ready, [3] for you are still of the flesh. For while there is jealousy and strife among you, are you not of the flesh, and behaving like ordinary men? [4] For when one says, "I belong to Paul," and another, "I belong to Apol'los," are you not merely men?

[5] What then is Apol'los? What is Paul? Servants through whom you believed, as the Lord assigned to each. [6] I planted, Apol'los watered, but God gave the growth. [7] So neither he who plants nor he who waters is anything, but only God who gives the growth. [8] He who plants and he who waters are equal, and each shall receive his wages according to his labor. [9] For we are God's fellow workers; you are God's field, God's building.

Why did Paul compare the Corinthian Christians to "infants in Christ" (1 Corinthians 3:1)? What made them less like spiritual adults and more like babies, not ready for solid food? Paul could identify their immaturity in the fact that they were beginning to divide into factions claiming allegiance to different ministers of the gospel—Paul, Apollos, Peter, even Jesus himself (3:4; 1:12).

It seems that the Corinthians failed to recognize that the new life they received came from God, not from any one of his servants. Their fixation on particular ministers was paradoxical, since all those who preached the gospel to them had the same goal—to bring them to Christ and strengthen them in the life God had given to them.

How could the Corinthians have been so immature? Paul himself had lived with them for eighteen months, building them up and developing an intimate rapport with them (Acts 18:11). Then Apollos—an articulate and prayerful man—had come to care for them (18:24–19:1). Throughout this time, the Corinthians experienced the power of the Spirit working in and among them (1 Corinthians 1:4-7). Perhaps enthusiasm for their gifted teachers blinded them to the fundamental reality that their life came from God and not from their teachers (3:6-7).

Paul made use of this troublesome situation to teach the Corinthians an important lesson. The way to deepen our Christian life and serve the kingdom of God is to bow to the Lord as the source of our life and to go directly to him for wisdom and comfort. Our spiritual life is not dependent on the people from whom we have received the gospel—gifted through they may be—but on the indwelling Holy Spirit. As we cultivate a relationship of prayerful and loving obedience with the Lord and allow his Spirit to free us from our sin, divisions among us will fade. We will grow up into strong and effective men and women of God, whose prayer and loving service advance the kingdom of heaven here on earth.

"Loving Father, I surrender my life to you, the giver of all life. Forgive me for allowing divisions to arise in my heart. Inflame me with love for you and draw me into a deeper communion with you."

1 Corinthians 3:10-15

[10] According to the grace of God given to me, like a skilled master builder I laid a foundation, and another man is building upon it. Let each man take care how he builds upon it. [11] For no other foundation can any one lay than that which is laid, which is Jesus Christ. [12] Now if any one builds on the foundation with gold, silver, precious stones, wood, hay, straw — [13] each man's work will become manifest; for the Day will disclose it, because it will be revealed with fire, and the fire will test what sort of work each one has done. [14] If the work which any man has built on the foundation survives, he will receive a reward. [15] If any man's work is burned up, he will suffer loss, though he himself will be saved, but only as through fire.

The young man phoned his mother with a plaintive question. "What went wrong?" A few days before, eager to display his cooking skills by fixing his buddies a nice meal, he had called for some favorite recipes. To his great disappointment, the meal had been only so-so. Mom quickly unearthed the problem: poor quality ingredients and emergency substitutions. Not even the good foundation of her time-tested recipes could rescue dishes built from tired vegetables and imitation chocolate.

When St. Paul urged the Corinthians to build carefully on a solid foundation (1 Corinthians 3:10), he wasn't targeting construction workers—or master chefs! Of course, his words apply to the attitude we should take as we go about our ordinary tasks in the kitchen, at the office, and everywhere else. But first of all, Paul's warning should stimulate us to reflect seriously on the overall picture of what we are building through our activities.

Jesus calls each of us to make some unique contribution to the temple of God, the church. The question is: As we seek to fulfill this mission of advancing God's kingdom, are we building on the firm foundation that has already been laid (1 Corinthians 3:11)? A related question has to do with approach: Are we building with care and with materials that befit the foundation? No construction project done with low-grade lumber and slipshod workmanship will stand the tests of time and scrutiny. Neither will any poorly executed work for God (3:12-15).

Which Christians make good builders of God's temple? Those who are careful and conscientious, Paul told the Corinthians. Those who avoid rivalry, humbly relying on God and doing everything for his glory (1 Corinthians 3:3-10; 10:31). Joy and wholeheartedness are important as well, "for God loves a cheerful giver" (2 Corinthians 9:7).

Among the many other qualities that Paul mentions in his letters, one that ranks high is contentment with the particular kind of service or spiritual gift God has given you. If you're a foot in Christ's body, says Paul, be the best foot you can be and don't aim to be a hand (1 Corinthians 12:14-30)! If you're a gutter in Christ's temple, be zealous about doing the job right and don't aspire to be a window! Or, to borrow another example from the kitchen, don't feel unimportant because your task is to prepare the appetizers instead of the main course! Put your energy, time, and talent into following God's directions for making those appetizers superb. When the day of the heavenly banquet arrives, you will not be disappointed.

"Jesus, I want to be careful and faithful, cheerful and content as I work to advance your kingdom today. Please show me what to do and how to rely on you as I do it."

1 Corinthians 3:16-17

[16] Do you not know that you are God's temple and that God's Spirit dwells in you? [17] If any one destroys God's temple, God will destroy him. For God's temple is holy, and that temple you are.

In the ancient world, desecration of a temple was a capital crime. The Greek word for temple, which derives from the verb "to reside," indicates why: Damage to a sacred site was considered a sacrilegious offense against the god or goddess who was thought to dwell there. Many people believed that the gods avenged such crimes themselves!

St. Paul and the members of the Christian community in Corinth took a different view. Most of the Corinthian Christians were Greek converts who had once worshipped at the city's pagan shrines. They had come to believe in the one true God, who "does not live in sanctuaries made by human hands" (Acts 17:24). As Paul forcefully reminded them, God does have a dwelling place on earth, but it is not a building of mortar and stone: You are it! he told them. "You are God's temple. . . . God's Spirit dwells in you" (1 Corinthians 3:16).

Imagine, for a moment, that you are hearing Paul's words for the first time. Take them personally. Let them sink in. "You are God's temple." Because the Holy Spirit began his life in you at baptism, you are holy. Every part of you is consecrated to God and belongs to him in a special way. The glorious Creator of heaven and earth has chosen to live in you! The God of love who sent his own Son to redeem the world has made his home in you! Are you living in a way that expresses who you really are—a temple of the Holy Spirit?

Because St. Paul especially wanted to underline the fact that the Christian community as a whole is the temple of God, you should also ask yourself: "Do you not know . . . that God's Spirit dwells among you?" The Corinthians needed some reminding on this point, since they were prone to jealous quarrels and rivalries (1 Corinthians 3:3-4). We too need to be reminded from time to time about this community dimension of God's temple. Consider, for example, whether you are relating to your parish in a way that respects and furthers God's plan to build a people in whom his Spirit lives. Do you shun divisive criticism, bickering, and backbiting? When you disagree, do you try to do so in a way that preserves unity?

"God's temple is holy, and that temple you are" (3:17). Today, take this verse as your guide for the way you think about and treat yourself and your brothers and sisters in Christ. Let the Spirit shine out from God's temple to the whole world!

"Lord Jesus, may the light of your life illumine every Christian and your entire church. As you once cleansed your Father's house in Jerusalem, cleanse us of all impurities. Make us worthy to be the temple of your Holy Spirit."

1 Corinthians 3:18-23

[18] Let no one deceive himself. If any one among you thinks that he is wise in this age, let him become a fool that he may become wise. [19] For the wisdom of this world is folly with God. For it is written, "He catches the wise in their craftiness," [20] and again, "The Lord knows that the thoughts of the wise are futile." [21] So let no one boast of men. For all things are yours, [22] whether Paul or Apol'los or

Cephas or the world or life or death or the present or the future, all are yours; [23] and you are Christ's; and Christ is God's.

Paul told the Corinthians that union with Christ would result in their being looked upon as fools according to the standards of the world. Two thousand years later, we can still see how heeding Paul's advice can mean making choices that are incomprehensible—or even foolish—to those who have not opened their hearts to the Lord.

How contrary is the wisdom of the cross to the wisdom of the world! In the Sermon on the Mount, Jesus said that the pure, the meek, the merciful, and the poor in spirit were the blessed ones (Matthew 5:3-10). The world, on the other hand, applauds the self-indulgent, the immoral, the rich, and the powerful.

Speaking about herself and her sisters, Mother Teresa of Calcutta once said: "To the world, we are wasting precious life and burying our talents. Yes, our lives are utterly wasted if we use only the light of reason. Our life has no meaning unless we look at Christ in his poverty. . . . We have nothing to live on, yet we live splendidly; nothing to walk on, yet we walk fearlessly; nothing to lean on, but yet we lean on God confidently; for we are his own and he is our provident Father" (*Jesus, the Word to Be Spoken*, pp. 87,88).

An old proverb states that the only way to knowledge is to confess our ignorance, and the only way to become wise is to realize we are fools. A Christian restatement of this proverb would be to say that a fool is one humble enough to be taught by God. It is the Holy Spirit who enables us to put God's word into action by bringing it to life within our hearts. God's thoughts are not our thoughts; his ways are not our ways (Isaiah 55:8). Yet in his love, he has revealed his wisdom, his plan of salvation through Christ.

By the power of the Spirit, we can learn from God; we can be formed by him; we can become like him. His ways may call for us to take an unpopular course, or to change some of our ways. But this is the way of discipleship, and its goal is nothing less than union with Christ. As we accept the "folly" of Christianity, let us rely on the promise that all things are ours, and we are Christ's (1 Corinthians 3:23). This is our great heritage. Let us embrace it.

1 Corinthians 4:1-8

[1] This is how one should regard us, as servants of Christ and stewards of the mysteries of God. [2] Moreover it is required of stewards that they be found trustworthy. [3] But with me it is a very small thing that I should be judged by you or by any human court. I do not even judge myself. [4] I am not aware of anything against myself, but I am not thereby acquitted. It is the Lord who judges me. [5] Therefore do not pronounce judgment before the time, before the Lord comes, who will bring to light the things now hidden in darkness and will disclose the purposes of the heart. Then every man will receive his commendation from God.

[6] I have applied all this to myself and Apol'los for your benefit, brethren, that you may learn by us not to go beyond what is written, that none of you may be puffed up in favor of one against another. [7] For who sees anything different in you? What have you that you did not receive? If then you received it, why do you boast as if it were not a gift?

[8] Already you are filled! Already you have become rich! Without us you have become kings! And would that you did reign, so that we might share the rule with you!

When Paul urged his readers to be "servants" of Christ and "stewards" of God's mysteries (1 Corinthians 4:1), he did not use the usual Greek words for these terms. For servants, he used *hyperetes*, which referred to the bottom row of galley rowers, the lowest of the low, an underling. For stewards, he used *oikonomos*, the term reserved for subordinate managers of other people's property who had none of their own.

Paul was intent on teaching that serving Christ and being good stewards in the church require always taking the lowest place. Had not Jesus himself said: "I am among you as one who serves" (Luke 22:27)? Paul was an unusually gifted man, yet he considered himself a servant and steward of Christ.

What does all this have to do with us, centuries later? Perhaps we could examine our consciences to see what our attitudes are toward service. Too often we are willing to serve provided that we are put in charge of the operation. We want to serve as masters rather than, like Paul, as a servant—indeed, as a slave. We frequently want to be in charge so that we can be in control and do things our way. We may rationalize that we only want to use the gifts God gave us, but in reality we simply don't like to take orders—from anyone. The gifts we claim to be using often are the fruit of worldly wisdom rather than wisdom flowing from God.

A prime characteristic of stewards and servants is that they be trustworthy (1 Corinthians 4:2). How do we measure our trustworthiness? By the level of our education, intelligence, professional training, experience? Or by our obedience to Jesus and faithfulness to all he teaches? In the context of this passage, we are trustworthy to the extent that we are (like Christ) a servant to others. This attitude does not come naturally, but by the work of Jesus in our hearts. Only he can give us hearts that want to be servants and stewards.

"Lord Jesus, you came among us as one who serves. You know my heart and its tendency to lord it over others. Make my heart like yours. Let me know the joy of serving in humility, as you did."

1 Corinthians 4:9-15

[9] For I think that God has exhibited us apostles as last of all, like men sentenced to death; because we have become a spectacle to the world, to angels and to men. [10] We are fools for Christ's sake, but you are wise in Christ. We are weak, but you are strong. You are held in honor, but we in disrepute. [11] To the present hour we hunger and thirst, we are ill-clad and buffeted and homeless, [12] and we labor, working with our own hands. When reviled, we bless; when persecuted, we endure; [13] when slandered, we try to conciliate; we have become, and are now, as the refuse of the world, the offscouring of all things.

[14] I do not write this to make you ashamed, but to admonish you as my beloved children. [15] For though you have countless guides in Christ, you do not have many fathers. For I became your father in Christ Jesus through the gospel.

How often Scripture reminds us of the love the Father has for each one of us! Yet, when it comes to the issue of our love for him, it always seems to come through a question that we alone must answer, or through a parable that Jesus poses. Remember the question to Peter after the resurrection, "Simon, son of John, do you love me more than these?" (John 21:15), or the parable of the pearl of great price (Matthew 13:45-46)?

The images are strikingly simple, but the challenge is immense. Of course it is vital that each of us accepts the Father's unconditional love for us. But if we want that love to grow, it is just as crucial that we give up those things that hinder our walk with the Lord. We are called not only to believe, but also to live by faith in the one who has touched our hearts.

The Corinthians had joyfully accepted the gospel but were reluctant to take up the life of faith that could deepen their experience of Jesus' presence. The thought of being held in lesser esteem by their neighbors, or of putting to death the fallen drives toward self-advancement, loomed too large in their minds. Whereas Paul and his companions willingly accepted the possibility of being "fools for Christ's sake," the Corinthians preferred being "held in honor" by their unbelieving friends (1 Corinthians 4:10). As a result, not only did they miss out on greater blessings from the Lord, they fell into rivalry, mistrust, and pride.

We have the same opportunity set before us today. We can look past whatever challenges lie ahead and embrace the goal of our faith: life with Christ beginning right now and enduring for all eternity. Do not be put off by the challenges of living for Jesus today. Embrace them. Remember, it was for you that he came and died. The same Holy Spirit that raised Jesus from the dead is ready to lead you closer to your Father in heaven.

"Heavenly Father, I praise you for offering me a share in your *agapé* love. Thank you, Lord Jesus, for dying for me so that I could live in you. Holy Spirit, you are my only hope for a deeper life with Christ. Stay close to me this day."

1 Corinthians 4:16-21

[16] I urge you, then, be imitators of me. [17] Therefore I sent to you Timothy, my beloved and faithful child in the Lord, to remind you of my ways in Christ, as I teach them everywhere in every church. [18] Some are arrogant, as though I were not coming to you. [19] But I will come to you soon, if the Lord wills, and I will find out not the talk of these arrogant people but their power. [20] For the kingdom of God does not consist in talk but in power. [21] What do you wish? Shall I come to you with a rod, or with love in a spirit of gentleness?

Paul was on his second missionary journey when, in the town of Lystra, he met Timothy for the first time (Acts 16:1-5). The young man came highly recommended by other members of the local church. Paul apparently agreed with their assessment, since he invited Timothy to join him in spreading the gospel. The apostle probably didn't know that his relationship with this rookie would prove to be a major support and consolation amid the hardships of his missionary calling. But over time, Timothy became such a faithful "imitator" of his teacher—who was himself such a faithful "imitator" of

Christ (1 Corinthians 4:16; 11:1)—that he earned Paul's total trust. Whenever Paul was unable to visit particular churches, he sent Timothy as his personal emissary to "remind you of my ways in Christ, as I teach them everywhere in every church" (4:17).

But this was not just a pragmatic business relationship. As they worked together, Paul and Timothy developed a deep mutual affection. Paul called Timothy "my beloved and faithful child in the Lord" (1 Corinthians 4:17). In another letter, he observed that Timothy was assisting him "as a son with a father" (Philippians 2:22). Elsewhere, Timothy is described as "our brother and God's servant in the gospel of Christ" (1 Thessalonians 3:2). What Timothy thought of Paul has not come down to us in so many words, but his actions indicate that he was no less appreciative.

Paul and Timothy were not just devoted friends; they were brothers—members of the family gathered to God by its "firstborn" brother, Jesus Christ (Romans 8:29). Since we too are part of this multitude of brothers and sisters, we also have the opportunity to develop strong, supportive relationships with one another. By learning to relate as brothers and sisters in the Lord, we can inspire one another to more loving, faithful service of God and neighbor. We can offer and receive wise advice, good example, prayer, encouragement, and that occasional eye-opening word of correction.

If you have already experienced this brotherhood and sisterhood in your own Christian life, you can easily add to this list of blessings. And if you have not, why not ask the Lord to help you enter into the experience of Christ-centered friendship? You can be sure that such a prayer is in accord with the will of the Father, who wants to see all his children drawn together in the same burning love that unites the Trinity.

"Father, thank you for sending your Son into the world to gather a family to yourself. Jesus, help me to love my brothers and sisters as you love them—and me. Holy Spirit, open my eyes to new opportunities for friendship with other members of God's family, even those I might not normally consider my type."

Divisions and Disputes

1 Corinthians 5:1–11:1

1 Corinthians 5:1-8

[1] It is actually reported that there is immorality among you, and of a kind that is not found even among pagans; for a man is living with his father's wife. [2] And you are arrogant! Ought you not rather to mourn? Let him who has done this be removed from among you.
[3] For though absent in body I am present in spirit, and as if present, I have already pronounced judgment [4] in the name of the Lord Jesus on the man who has done such a thing. When you are assembled, and my spirit is present, with the power of our Lord Jesus, [5] you are to deliver this man to Satan for the destruction of the flesh, that his spirit may be saved in the day of the Lord Jesus.
[6] Your boasting is not good. Do you not know that a little leaven leavens the whole lump? [7] Cleanse out the old leaven that you may be a new lump, as you really are unleavened. For Christ, our paschal lamb, has been sacrificed. [8] Let us, therefore, celebrate the festival, not with the old leaven, the leaven of malice and evil, but with the unleavened bread of sincerity and truth.

"No Big Deal." That's the attitude the Corinthian Christians seem to have taken toward one of their community members committing incest. Some Corinthians, inflated with pride and impressed that they were already living a "supernatural" life, were boasting of their spiritual experiences. They thought their "mature" knowledge transcended ethical norms, and so they took an "enlightened" view of morality. Apparently, they had misunderstood freedom in Christ to mean freedom to do anything.

It seems these attitudes troubled Paul almost as much as the sin itself. He knew that "a little leaven leavens the whole lump" (1 Corinthians 5:6), and was concerned that this case of incest was not an isolated incident but was a symptom of a wider problem. In treating this offense so lightly, the Corinthians showed that they had lost sight of the holiness of God and had begun considering themselves capable of deciding on their own what kinds of behavior they should consider sinful.

We risk making the same mistake as the Corinthians when we look to our feelings and spiritual experiences as the only measures of our holiness. God loves to give us freedom and revelation, but he also calls us to measure our hearts and our behavior against his commandments. We need to remember that, whatever our experience of the Christian life may be, the law of the Lord will never pass away (Matthew 5:18).

This is why examination of conscience is so important. Until the day when Jesus returns in glory, temptation will be a part of our lives, and so we must remain ever vigilant. We all know how easy it can be to minimize our sin, or to make excuses for our weaknesses.

Every day, allow the Holy Spirit to search your heart. Every day, ask him to show you how you have sinned against God, those around you, and even yourself. Let Jesus cover you with his mercy and free you more and more from sin. The call to holiness and purity is not a call to do the impossible. It's a call to become what we already are—a new creation in Christ Jesus.

"Come, Holy Spirit, and search my heart. Teach me to guard my ways according to your commands. May I never stray from you and the love that you have poured into me."

1 Corinthians 5:9-13

[9] I wrote to you in my letter not to associate with immoral men; [10] not at all meaning the immoral of this world, or the greedy and robbers, or idolaters, since then you would need to go out of the world. [11] But rather I wrote to you not to associate with any one who bears the name of brother if he is guilty of immorality or greed, or is an idolater, reviler, drunkard, or robber — not even to eat with such a one. [12] For what have I to do with judging outsiders? Is it not those inside the church whom you are to judge? [13] God judges those outside. "Drive out the wicked person from among you."

How can Christians live as the Lord's followers in the world without compromising their beliefs and becoming of the world? This is a frequent theme in Paul's letters. The subject under discussion in this passage, however, hits somewhat closer to home. Paul is talking about how to be in—and truly of—the church.

The question would never arise if Jesus had intended his disciples to form a "spiritual" club with no connection to everyday life and no impact on it. But the church is not like a giant movie theater or vacation hideaway where people can indulge in escapist activities to forget about the real world! The church is more like a good home—a community that helps its members to grow in maturity so that they can go out into the world knowing and doing what is right. This means that the church itself must provide a social environment that supports right living.

The church in Corinth was shooting itself in the foot by tolerating members who were repeat—and unrepentant—offenders against God's law (1 Corinthians 5:11). No stream will flow clean and pure if it is polluted at its source. No church community can give a clear witness to the world or a good example to its own members if it condones the behavior of people who call themselves Christians while engaging in serious sin. This is why Paul warns the Corinthians not to associate with these wolves in sheep's clothing (5:11). He even urges that they be driven out of the Christian community (5:13).

But let none of us start drawing up lists of people we would like to see expelled from our local church communities! Instead of finger-pointing, we should take Paul's words as an incentive to do some soul-searching: "Am I fostering a healthy social environment in the church?" Take a few minutes to ask yourself specific questions along these lines:

- Are my thoughts, words, and deeds in line with Christ's teaching?

- Do I acknowledge and confess my sins and seek God's help for change in areas of weakness?

- Have I been tolerating sinful habits or rationalizing them away because I don't want to give them up?

- Do I follow and defend the church's teaching? What am I doing to understand it better?

- Does the way I speak about the church and its members build up or tear down?

"Lord, I want to expel—from my own self—everything that undermines the common life of your family. Help me to live fully for you and to help my brothers and sisters do the same."

1 Corinthians 6:1-11

1 When one of you has a grievance against a brother, does he dare go to law before the unrighteous instead of the saints? 2 Do you not know that the saints will judge the world? And if the world is to be judged by you, are you incompetent to try trivial cases? 3 Do you not know that we are to judge angels? How much more, matters pertaining to this life! 4 If then you have such cases, why do you lay them before those who are least esteemed by the church? 5 I say this to your shame. Can it be that there is no man among you wise enough to decide between members of the brotherhood, 6 but brother goes to law against brother, and that before unbelievers?

7 To have lawsuits at all with one another is defeat for you. Why not rather suffer wrong? Why not rather be defrauded? 8 But you yourselves wrong and defraud, and that even your own brethren.

9 Do you not know that the unrighteous will not inherit the kingdom of God? Do not be deceived; neither the immoral, nor idolaters, nor adulterers, nor sexual perverts, 10 nor thieves, nor the greedy, nor drunkards, nor revilers, nor robbers will inherit the kingdom of God. 11 And such were some of you. But you were washed, you were sanctified, you were justified in the name of the Lord Jesus Christ and in the Spirit of our God.

After confronting the Corinthians on immoral practices, Paul took dead aim at their lawsuits between believers. The Corinthians went too far in thinking that since they were in Christ and "dead to the law," they could continue in sin. So Paul asked three times "Do you not know?" to emphasize for them the difference between real Christianity and the life they were leading!

The question is a good one for all of us to ask. Do you not know that the gospel is "the power of God for salvation to everyone who has faith" (Romans 1:16)? Do you not know that you were washed, sanctified, and justified in the name of the Lord Jesus Christ (1 Corinthians 6:11)? Do you not know that you can "put off your old nature" and "put on the new nature, created after the likeness of God" (Ephesians 4:22,24)?

Losing sight of the power of the gospel not only brings down our lives, it influences everyone around us. One lapse leads to another, until we wonder how it ever got so bad. For the Corinthians, Paul had to remind them that they now belonged to Christ. Yes, they were washed and justified, but they were also sanctified, which means separated out for God. If they had thought about being united with Christ, they would have held themselves to a higher standard.

It is equally true that when we are in touch with the gospel as revealed by the Spirit, beautiful and miraculous things can happen. We are confident that the power of the resurrection is at work in us and in every believer. This truth alone can transform us to the degree that others would see a change in us. The freedom and power of the saints' lives are often attributed to their confidence in God and their openness to the Holy Spirit. The gospel brings fullness of life, not just more of the same old life. Let's lift our hearts to the Lord and ask for greater revelation of all that is ours in Christ.

"Thank you, Father, for revealing the gospel of power, transformation, and freedom from sin. Give me grace to live in the fullness of this gospel and not wander from your promises."

1 Corinthians 6:12-20

[12] "All things are lawful for me," but not all things are helpful. "All things are lawful for me," but I will not be enslaved by anything. [13] "Food is meant for the stomach and the stomach for food" — and God will destroy both one and the other. The body is not meant for immorality, but for the Lord, and the Lord for the body. [14] And God raised the Lord and will also raise us up by his power. [15] Do you not know that your bodies are members of Christ? Shall I therefore take the members of Christ and make them members of a prostitute? Never! [16] Do you not know that he who joins himself to a prostitute becomes one body with her? For, as it is written, "The two shall become one." [17] But he who is united to the Lord becomes one spirit with him. [18] Shun immorality. Every other sin which a man commits is outside the body; but the immoral man sins against his own body. [19] Do you not know that your body is a temple of the Holy Spirit within you, which you have from God? You are not your own; [20] you were bought with a price. So glorify God in your body.

*"Yeah, I watch off-color television shows sometimes—
but strictly for laughs. I rise above that stuff. It doesn't affect me."*

"The body is like a prison. To be really pure and spiritual, you have to disregard it and look down on this lowly material world."

If St. Paul were to overhear comments like these, he wouldn't let them pass uncorrected. In fact, he didn't let them pass! In modern terms, these statements express some of the thinking that Paul encountered among the Corinthian Christians. "All things are lawful for me" (1 Corinthians 6:12) was apparently a slogan that some of them were invoking to justify their immoral behavior. Influenced by the popular philosophies of their day, these Christians had adopted the view that the body is too weak and base to play any role in the spiritual life. To their way of thinking, only the spirit mattered—and it was far too pure and exalted to be affected by any action carried out "in the body."

Paul corrected this mistaken idea in no uncertain terms, and in a way that helps us sort out these issues as they arise today. He took a holistic approach, viewing the person as a unified ensemble of the physical and the spiritual. What we do with our bodies is therefore very important and does indeed impact the spiritual dimension, Paul insisted.

Our bodies—and not just our minds and hearts—are "members of Christ" and belong to him (1 Corinthians 6:15,19). We can't compartmentalize ourselves into one section marked "for the Lord" and another marked "for me." Maybe you lived that way once, says Paul, but that's over now! "The body is not meant for immorality, but for the Lord, and the Lord for the body" (6:13). The conclusion is clear: "So glorify God in your body" (6:20).

As you think about how to respond to Paul's instruction, try reflecting some more on his image of the body as a temple of the

Holy Spirit (1 Corinthians 6:19; 3:16-17). A temple or church is sacred space. It is a place where God makes himself present in a special way, a place with a pattern of worship and prayer. Your body is "sacred space" too. Do you cultivate an openness to meeting God there? Do you treat your body with the care and respect it deserves? Are you developing patterns and habits of prayer and offering that help you to worship and glorify God?

Today, ask the Lord to reveal and help you change anything about the way you relate to your body that hinders your ability to see yourself as his temple. Ask him to help you to love him with your whole self. Throw open all the doors, and welcome the adventure of learning to "glorify God with your body"!

1 Corinthians 7:1-9

[1] Now concerning the matters about which you wrote. It is well for a man not to touch a woman. [2] But because of the temptation to immorality, each man should have his own wife and each woman her own husband. [3] The husband should give to his wife her conjugal rights, and likewise the wife to her husband. [4] For the wife does not rule over her own body, but the husband does; likewise the husband does not rule over his own body, but the wife does. [5] Do not refuse one another except perhaps by agreement for a season, that you may devote yourselves to prayer; but then come together again, lest Satan tempt you through lack of self-control. [6] I say this by way of concession, not of command. [7] I wish that all were as I myself am.

But each has his own special gift from God, one of one kind and one of another.

[8] To the unmarried and the widows I say that it is well for them to remain single as I do. [9] But if they cannot exercise self-control, they should marry. For it is better to marry than to be aflame with passion.

It seems that some members of the Corinthian church, most probably married women, thought Christians should be "above" sexual activity. Instead of giving in to their passions, they should devote their time to holier pursuits. As a result, they asserted the idea that it was better for a man not to "touch" a woman (a euphemism for sexual intercourse).

When Paul says spouses have "conjugal rights" to one another, we might think he is being rigid or legalistic. In reality, he's trying to capture a beautiful reality: Sexual love in marriage is an expression of mutual self-giving. It's not a matter of one spouse demanding something from the other. Rather, it's a matter of each spouse owing to the other the gift of himself or herself.

Pope John Paul II explored this theme in his book, *Love and Responsibility*: "Contrary to the superficial view of sex, according to which love (meaning here erotic love) culminates in a woman's surrender of her body to a man, we should rightly speak of the mutual surrender of both persons, of their belonging equally to each other. Not mutual sexual exploitation . . . but the reciprocated gift of self, so that two persons belong to each other" (Chapter II, Section 3). In this understanding, love leads a married person to want to surrender to his or her beloved. In Christian marriage, a spouse's body is not his or her own exclusive property, but the "property" of another. Because this is meant to be a mutual sense of love and self-giving, there is no risk involved. Both spouses view one another as persons not to be used as mere objects for sexual gratification but as persons created in God's image. What a privilege—and what a high calling! In every marriage, sexual love can actually reflect the mutual self-giving love of the Trinity!

Paul's words here go beyond the immediate issue of sexual love. They show that God wants to transform more than just our ideas about sexuality. He wants to transform our concepts about all aspects of our lives. We can love others and give the gift of ourselves in many ways, and all of them are rooted in the gifts which we have first received from God through the Holy Spirit. In marriage, in our families, in our neighborhoods, and in our church, we are called to love with the love God has for us. In all these avenues, we are called to give of ourselves, because he has first given himself to us.

"Lord, the reality of your plan for married love is more beautiful and satisfying than any worldly philosophy. Change my view of love and enable me to give of myself just as you have given yourself to me!"

1 Corinthians 7:10-16

[10] To the married I give charge, not I but the Lord, that the wife should not separate from her husband [11] (but if she does, let her remain single or else be reconciled to her husband) — and that the husband should not divorce his wife.

[12] To the rest I say, not the Lord, that if any brother has a wife who is an unbeliever, and she consents to live with him, he should not divorce her. [13] If any woman has a husband who is an unbeliever, and he consents to live with her, she should not divorce him. [14] For the unbelieving husband is consecrated through his wife, and the unbelieving wife is consecrated through her husband. Otherwise, your children would be unclean, but as it is they are holy. [15] But if the unbelieving partner desires to separate, let it be so; in such a case the brother or sister is not bound. For God has called us to peace. [16] Wife, how do you know whether you will save your husband? Husband, how do you know whether you will save your wife?

It's likely that we know, either directly or indirectly, at least one family broken by divorce. The reasons for the divorce may be understandable, such as abuse or infidelity, or they may be mystifying. Either way, we might wish that Paul had stayed away from the topic, knowing the pain and suffering that often accompanies the disintegration of a marriage.

But Paul never avoided emotionally charged issues, precisely because he understood the power of the gospel and the goodness of God's intentions. Much more than a contract, marriage is a vocation or calling in which believers mirror the self-giving love of God and help each other become more holy. As each person gives himself or herself in love to the other, willingly rooting out the causes of division, they both grow closer to one another and to God. Research, as well as common sense, has shown that couples committed to living this ideal are the least likely to suffer the pain of divorce.

It's interesting that Paul urges couples to stay together even if one spouse is not a believer. Some of us may wonder why, especially considering the vastly different outlooks that can result when one spouse has so radically different an outlook on life than the other. But Paul understood that marriage can communicate sanctifying grace. The believing spouse can be a witness to the unbeliever, not by nagging or "preaching" but by virtue of his or her holiness—by virtue of the way he or she loves God and (as a result) his or her spouse. Faithfulness to the Christian ideal of married life, even of one spouse, gives the Holy Spirit plenty of room to transform the union and pour out blessing upon the entire family.

Imagine a devout young woman married to a young lawyer. Within a few years, her husband was unfaithful. He amassed debts for which she had to sell all of her belongings, and the family was forced to move in with his parents. Eventually, she was forced to take an apartment in poverty with her two young children. If she chose to end her marriage, everyone would understand. But she didn't. She remained faithful both to her spiritual life and to her husband. Her witness was so strong that her husband turned his life around and gave his heart to Jesus. Though Blessed Elisabetta Canori Mora suffered deeply in her marriage, she saw her faithfulness rewarded far beyond what most people would expect. Through her patience, love, and intercession, her husband was transformed.

"Holy Spirit, I praise you for your power to transform each person's life. Your desire for unity can overcome even the biggest obstacles!"

1 Corinthians 7:17-24

[17] Only, let every one lead the life which the Lord has assigned to him, and in which God has called him. This is my rule in all the churches. [18] Was any one at the time of his call already circumcised? Let him not seek to remove the marks of circumcision. Was any one at the time of his call uncircumcised? Let him not seek circumcision. [19] For neither circumcision counts for anything nor uncircumcision, but keeping the commandments of God. [20] Every one should remain in the state in which he was called. [21] Were you a slave when called? Never mind. But if you can gain your freedom, avail yourself of the opportunity. [22] For he who was called in the Lord as a slave is a freedman of the Lord. Likewise he who was free when called is a slave of Christ. [23] You were bought with a price; do not become slaves of men. [24] So, brethren, in whatever state each was called, there let him remain with God.

Elbow-deep in soapsuds, washing dishes after a chaotic breakfast, with two children's diapers left to change, children to dress and load into a van, a mother could think that her life would be much better if she retreated to a quiet religious community and devoted her time to uninterrupted prayer. After all, wouldn't she become a lot more holy there, and become even more effective in God's kingdom? But to this young mother, and to the Corinthians as well, Paul says: "Remain as you are."

Some of the Christians in Corinth wanted to pursue super-spiritual occupations, and in pursuit of this goal, they began to look down on more mundane ways of life. They sought what they thought were obvious trappings of spiritual maturity, signs that they were holier than others. But Paul stops them short, telling them that their situation, in and of itself, has no spiritual significance. The key to holiness and spiritual effectiveness is allowing the grace of conversion to transform our situation, wherever we find ourselves!

Paul's thoughts echo throughout the Vatican II document *Dogmatic Constitution on the Church.* In that document, the Council Fathers taught that all lay people are called to "seek the kingdom of God by engaging in temporal affairs and by ordering them according to the plan of God" (31). In other words, in the ordinary circumstances of family, work, and social life, lay people have a powerful opportunity to sanctify the world from within—just as a little bit of yeast can affect a large amount of dough (Matthew 13:33). "Consequently," the Fathers taught, "even when preoccupied with temporal cares, the laity can and must perform a work of great value for the evangelization of the world" (35).

The key is that, wherever we are, we remain with God. In our ordinary lives, we can make a great difference for his kingdom. We grow in holiness as we offer every struggle, decision, or sacrifice to God. Our lives are transformed, and we shine as a light to everyone around us. Each one of us is irreplaceable. Each one of us has a vital role to play, right where we are. We do not have to wait—we can make a difference starting today!

"Thank you, Jesus! I do not have to be doing something super-holy to be your follower. I just have to be faithful where I am. No one else can take my place, and you have put me here so you can use me to change this world!"

1 Corinthians 7:25-40

[25] Now concerning the unmarried, I have no command of the Lord, but I give my opinion as one who by the Lord's mercy is trustworthy. [26] I think that in view of the present distress it is well for a person to remain as he is. [27] Are you bound to a wife? Do not seek to be free. Are you free from a wife? Do not seek marriage. [28] But if you marry, you do not sin, and if a girl marries she does not sin. Yet those who marry will have worldly troubles, and I would spare you that. [29] I mean, brethren, the appointed time has grown very short; from now on, let those who have wives live as though they had none, [30] and those who mourn as though they were not mourning, and those who rejoice as though they were not rejoicing, and those who buy as though they had no goods, [31] and those who deal with the world as though they had no dealings with it. For the form of this world is passing away.

[32] I want you to be free from anxieties. The unmarried man is anxious about the affairs of the Lord, how to please the Lord; [33] but the married man is anxious about worldly affairs, how to please his wife, [34] and his interests are divided. And the unmarried woman or girl is anxious about the affairs of the Lord, how to be holy in body and spirit; but the married woman is anxious about worldly affairs, how to please her husband. [35] I say this for your own benefit, not to lay any restraint upon you, but to promote good order and to secure your undivided devotion to the Lord.

[36] If any one thinks that he is not behaving properly toward his betrothed, if his passions are strong, and it has to be, let him do as he wishes: let them marry — it is no sin. [37] But whoever is firmly established in his heart, being under no necessity but having his desire under control, and has determined this in his heart, to keep

her as his betrothed, he will do well. [38] So that he who marries his betrothed does well; and he who refrains from marriage will do better. [39] A wife is bound to her husband as long as he lives. If the husband dies, she is free to be married to whom she wishes, only in the Lord. [40] But in my judgment she is happier if she remains as she is. And I think that I have the Spirit of God.

Imagine you are telling a joke to a group of friends. Only you know the punch line, and you are crafting the story carefully, in order to give the punch line the strongest effect. You don't get distracted by unrelated details, and you keep your attention on the end of the joke.

Paul urged the Corinthians to have this same focus on the end goal—except that he was talking about our salvation! And we already know the punch line. We already know that Jesus has defeated sin and death and that "this world is passing away" (1 Corinthians 7:31). We are destined for heaven! Of all people, we should be least likely to get bound up in things like social climbing or accumulating possessions.

The Corinthians needed a reminder to keep their heavenly perspective. Some of them even wanted to be admired so much that, in order to build up their sense of dignity and importance, they pursued consecrated or celibate lifestyles. But Paul reminded them to look to heaven, not to earth as they sought out the best way to live their newfound faith. Paul argued that since both the married and unmarried vocations are good, the only way to avoid anxieties is to embrace "undivided devotion to the Lord" (1 Corinthians 7:35), putting aside the world's way of looking at things and adopting the mind of Christ.

Living with a heavenly perspective is not about outward appearances, but motives. Bob's goal is to advance in his job and become director of his company. He longs for prestige, riches, and acclaim. Susan is very active in her church. She wants to impress the pastor and her fellow parishioners, and likes it when people admire her involvement. Of course, there is nothing wrong with being a corporate director, and we should all try to be involved in our local churches. But if Bob and Susan remain entrenched in earthly goals, they will lose their heavenly perspective.

God wants to give us the "big picture" so we can share his view. We have been redeemed! We are destined for heaven, to sit in glory with Jesus! We are children of God and have incomparable dignity! When we see every detail of our lives in light of these truths, it changes the way we approach each day: how we think, the choices we make, and the priorities we pursue. We know the "punch line," and it has become our hope and desire.

"Heavenly Father, draw my eyes upward to your throne. You have destined me for unspeakable glory with you! Let this truth transform all my motives."

1 Corinthians 8:1-13

[1] Now concerning food offered to idols: we know that "all of us possess knowledge." "Knowledge" puffs up, but love builds up. [2] If any one imagines that he knows something, he does not yet know as he ought to know. [3] But if one loves God, one is known by him.

[4] Hence, as to the eating of food offered to idols, we know that "an idol has no real existence," and that "there is no God but one." [5] For although there may be so-called gods in heaven or on earth — as

indeed there are many "gods" and many "lords" — [6] yet for us there is one God, the Father, from whom are all things and for whom we exist, and one Lord, Jesus Christ, through whom are all things and through whom we exist.

[7] However, not all possess this knowledge. But some, through being hitherto accustomed to idols, eat food as really offered to an idol; and their conscience, being weak, is defiled. [8] Food will not commend us to God. We are no worse off if we do not eat, and no better off if we do. [9] Only take care lest this liberty of yours somehow become a stumbling block to the weak. [10] For if any one sees you, a man of knowledge, at table in an idol's temple, might he not be encouraged, if his conscience is weak, to eat food offered to idols? [11] And so by your knowledge this weak man is destroyed, the brother for whom Christ died. [12] Thus, sinning against your brethren and wounding their conscience when it is weak, you sin against Christ. [13] Therefore, if food is a cause of my brother's falling, I will never eat meat, lest I cause my brother to fall.

In the ancient world, meat was not a dietary staple. It would have been available chiefly at public banquets that followed the ritual sacrifice of animals. For most people, the meat would have carried religious significance pertaining to those rites. Consequently, to eat meat sacrificed to idols was to acknowledge the religious implications of the pagan feast. Some "enlightened" Corinthian Christians maintained, however, that since idols did not exist, no harm could come from eating meat offered to them. Their position scandalized other believers, creating doubt, confusion, and misunderstanding in others who were not as knowledgeable.

Who was right? Strictly speaking, the "enlightened" Christians were. Paul acknowledged their reasoning: "As to the eating of food offered to idols, we know that 'an idol has no real existence,' and that 'there is no God but one'" (1 Corinthians 8:4). Belief in Jesus, however, is not a matter of knowledge and legalities, but of love. Our highest knowledge, Paul chides the "enlightened" ones, is not, and never will be, the knowledge possible through reason. There is something far better—love.

Mere knowledge of right or wrong, acceptable or unacceptable can inflate the ego and convey a false sense of righteousness. Although the "enlightened" ones may have been objectively correct, they erred, sinning against love by offending the consciences of the "weaker" Christians. In doing so, they created division among those called by God to be brothers and sisters in Christ—the antithesis of love, which unites.

Love has primacy over everything in our Christian lives—over knowledge, position, power, and gifts (1 Corinthians 13:1-13). "Love builds up" (8:1) and "binds everything together in perfect harmony" (Colossians 3:14). Paul answered those who considered it easier to pursue knowledge than love by stating that "if one loves God, one is known by him" (1 Corinthians 8:3). Our love comes from knowing God's love (1 John 4:19). The more we know his love, the more we will love others. Understanding Jesus' tender love for us, which grows ever deeper, will move us to place unity and mutual respect above knowledge, being "right" and keeping to the letter of the law.

God never tires of pouring out his love on us! Let us never tire of receiving it. As we receive his love, we can love others and build up the church on earth to the glory of the Father.

1 Corinthians 9:1-15

[1] Am I not free? Am I not an apostle? Have I not seen Jesus our Lord? Are not you my workmanship in the Lord? [2] If to others I am not an apostle, at least I am to you; for you are the seal of my apostleship in the Lord.

[3] This is my defense to those who would examine me. [4] Do we not have the right to our food and drink? [5] Do we not have the right to be accompanied by a wife, as the other apostles and the brothers of the Lord and Cephas? [6] Or is it only Barnabas and I who have no right to refrain from working for a living? [7] Who serves as a soldier at his own expense? Who plants a vineyard without eating any of its fruit? Who tends a flock without getting some of the milk?

[8] Do I say this on human authority? Does not the law say the same? [9] For it is written in the law of Moses, "You shall not muzzle an ox when it is treading out the grain." Is it for oxen that God is concerned? [10] Does he not speak entirely for our sake? It was written for our sake, because the plowman should plow in hope and the thresher thresh in hope of a share in the crop. [11] If we have sown spiritual good among you, is it too much if we reap your material benefits? [12] If others share this rightful claim upon you, do not we still more?

Nevertheless, we have not made use of this right, but we endure anything rather than put an obstacle in the way of the gospel of Christ. [13] Do you not know that those who are employed in the temple service get their food from the temple, and those who serve at the altar share in the sacrificial offerings? [14] In the same way, the Lord commanded that those who proclaim the gospel should get their living by the gospel.

[15] But I have made no use of any of these rights, nor am I writing this to secure any such provision. For I would rather die than have any one deprive me of my ground for boasting.

The next time you see a television commercial that urges you to grab for everything you can get or to indulge a desire because "you deserve it," you might reflect on the counterexample given by St. Paul. Here was a man who refused to put his own desires first—and even passed up opportunities to exercise his legitimate rights.

One of these was the right to receive material benefit from the work of preaching the gospel and establishing local churches. It's not that Paul thought it would be immoral to accept this kind of help. On the contrary, he offered arguments in favor of such support. He cited the example of other apostles, as well of the priests who served at the Jerusalem Temple (1 Corinthians 9:5, 12); he gave examples drawn from ordinary life (9:7); he quoted and interpreted a relevant Scripture passage (9:9-11). He even said it is a divine command that "those who proclaim the gospel should get their living by the gospel" (9:14)!

If Paul was so convinced that it was perfectly acceptable to receive material help, why did he refuse it? Why did he work to support himself by sewing and repairing tents and other canvas and leather goods (Acts 18:3)? Paul said only that he preferred to "endure anything rather than put an obstacle in the way of the gospel of Christ" (1 Corinthians 9:12). Perhaps he sensed that even accepting hospitality from some of the Corinthians might arouse jealousy or hinder his ability to serve the whole community equally.

Even though it meant a more difficult life, Paul passed up his rightful privileges in an exceptional way in order to serve the greater good. The same is true of the many servants of the gospel in the church today. We are all enriched by the witness of vowed religious, consecrated lay people, and others who forego their "rights" to marriage and financial independence by choosing the way of poverty and celibacy. We should pray for them regularly, asking God to make their generosity exceptionally fruitful for his kingdom.

We should also imitate their willingness to put other people's interests and welfare first. Applying this principle could mean deciding, for example, that "yes, I have a just claim on the inheritance, but I'd rather give it up than take my sister to court." It might mean choosing to help out in a medical clinic in Honduras instead of taking a cruise to the Bahamas. It might mean approaching retirement as an opportunity to spend more time volunteering in the parish and community than teeing off on the local golf course.

This sacrificial living brings true joy and freedom—and even, Paul would say, authentic grounds for a certain kind of boasting (1 Corinthians 9:15)!

"Lord, you are never outdone in generosity! I want to be more like you."

1 Corinthians 9:16-27

[16] For if I preach the gospel, that gives me no ground for boasting. For necessity is laid upon me. Woe to me if I do not preach the gospel! [17] For if I do this of my own will, I have a reward; but if not of my own will, I am entrusted with a commission. [18] What then is my reward? Just this: that in my preaching I may make the gospel free of charge, not making full use of my right in the gospel.

[19] For though I am free from all men, I have made myself a slave to all, that I might win the more. [20] To the Jews I became as a Jew, in order to win Jews; to those under the law I became as one under the law — though not being myself under the law — that I might win those under the law. [21] To those outside the law I became as one

outside the law — not being without law toward God but under the law of Christ — that I might win those outside the law. [22] To the weak I became weak, that I might win the weak. I have become all things to all men, that I might by all means save some. [23] I do it all for the sake of the gospel, that I may share in its blessings.

[24] Do you not know that in a race all the runners compete, but only one receives the prize? So run that you may obtain it. [25] Every athlete exercises self-control in all things. They do it to receive a perishable wreath, but we an imperishable. [26] Well, I do not run aimlessly, I do not box as one beating the air; [27] but I pommel my body and subdue it, lest after preaching to others I myself should be disqualified.

Paul was a man of such conviction and intense dedication to his calling to preach the gospel that he was ready to do anything to spread the good news. It was a compulsion: "For the love of Christ compels us" (2 Corinthians 5:14)—but one that did not rob him of his freedom. Actually, it freed him from lesser constraints so that he could fulfill the commission given him directly by Christ. What is it about preaching the gospel that provided such an irresistible motivation for Paul?

Many writers have commented on that question, but few with more eloquence than St. Lawrence of Brindisi:

> Preaching is an apostolic, angelic, Christian, and divine task. God's word is so rich that it is a treasury of every good. From it flow faith, hope, love, all the virtues, the many gifts of the Spirit, all the evangelical beatitudes, all good works and merits—the whole glory of paradise!

> God's word is light to the mind and fire to the will so that a person may know and love the Lord. To the interior person who lives by the Spirit it is bread and water, but a bread sweeter than honey from the comb, and water more delicious than milk or wine. (*Lenten Sermon*, 2)

Paul (and Lawrence!) recognized that the kingdom of God had broken into the world through Jesus Christ and that the word of God would bring life and salvation to all people who believed. Thus, he was impelled to proclaim the good news of Christ, for the salvation of the world depended on it.

God wants to fill each of us with this burning desire to proclaim the good news of salvation in Christ Jesus. While the clergy have a special calling to proclaim the gospel, lay people and religious brothers and sisters share in that role because they too "share in the priestly, prophetic, and royal office of Christ" (Vatican II, *The Apostolate of the Laity*, 2). All of us are invited—and all of us can be empowered—to share the good news of Jesus Christ, whether it be in the church, the home, or the workplace.

Only as Christ's love compels us will we be freed up to spread the gospel. Let us pray that we might know this love more deeply. May all of us, young and old alike, dedicate ourselves today to "proclaim the message; be persistent whether the time is favorable or unfavorable; convince, rebuke, and encourage, with the utmost patience in teaching" (2 Timothy 4:2).

1 Corinthians 10:1-13

[1] I want you to know, brethren, that our fathers were all under the cloud, and all passed through the sea, [2] and all were baptized into Moses in the cloud and in the sea, [3] and all ate the same supernatural food [4] and all drank the same supernatural drink. For they drank from the supernatural Rock which followed them, and the Rock was Christ. [5] Nevertheless with most of them God was not pleased; for they were overthrown in the wilderness.

[6] Now these things are warnings for us, not to desire evil as they did. [7] Do not be idolaters as some of them were; as it is written, "The people sat down to eat and drink and rose up to dance." [8] We must not indulge in immorality as some of them did, and twenty-three thousand fell in a single day. [9] We must not put the Lord to the test, as some of them did and were destroyed by serpents; [10] nor grumble, as some of them did and were destroyed by the Destroyer. [11] Now these things happened to them as a warning, but they were written down for our instruction, upon whom the end of the ages has come. [12] Therefore let any one who thinks that he stands take heed lest he fall. [13] No temptation has overtaken you that is not common to man. God is faithful, and he will not let you be tempted beyond your strength, but with the temptation will also provide the way of escape, that you may be able to endure it.

Because Paul had lived with the Corinthians for an extended period of time, he was able to speak openly to them about the difficulties that their church was having. Throughout this letter, Paul demonstrated that his greatest concern was division within the church, both division between believers and division within the hearts of individual believers.

When Paul addressed the issue of idolatry with the Corinthians, at the most basic level he was addressing the state of each believer's heart—whether their love and devotion to God was undivided or whether other things or people had taken places of greater honor or importance in their affections. The "idolaters" Paul describes in the Old Testament examples displeased the Lord because they did not follow him wholeheartedly. Yes, all the Israelites who left Egypt were under the cloud of his protection. Yes, they all passed safely through the Red Sea. Yes, they all drank from the same "spiritual rock" (Exodus 17:5-6). But still, after experiencing so many blessings from the Lord, many of them maintained a divided heart, and so they were not permitted to enter into the Promised Land.

It might be easy for us to dismiss Paul's examples here as "outdated," but the message is just as powerful for us today. Do we take idolatry seriously? If we don't, we risk missing out on how powerfully God wants to work in our lives. We are all tempted to seek material wealth, to make a good impression on other people, or to achieve success at the expense of our relationship with God or our families. Every day we face choices that will have an impact on each of these areas: Should I take the time out of my busy schedule to pray, or just get on with my day? Whose agenda and whose priorities will I put first? Will I take the time to listen to my neighbor who has had a rough day, or will I find a quick way to end the conversation?

As we ask the Holy Spirit to help us turn away from even the smallest tendency to put God in second place, a whole new realm opens up to us. Our faithfulness to the sacraments takes on a deeper meaning as we experience God's presence even more powerfully. Our efforts to remain committed to daily prayer and Scripture reading flower and bear fruit in our witness to others. We receive blessings we had not even foreseen!

"Lord God, help me to place you first. Let me not just go through the motions with my faith, having my mind preoccupied with the things of the world. Holy Spirit, uproot any traces of idolatry. I want a heart undivided in love for you!"

1 Corinthians 10:14-22

[14] Therefore, my beloved, shun the worship of idols. [15] I speak as to sensible men; judge for yourselves what I say. [16] The cup of blessing which we bless, is it not a participation in the blood of Christ? The bread which we break, is it not a participation in the body of Christ? [17] Because there is one bread, we who are many are one body, for we all partake of the one bread. [18] Consider the people of Israel; are not those who eat the sacrifices partners in the altar? [19] What do I imply then? That food offered to idols is anything, or that an idol is anything? [20] No, I imply that what pagans sacrifice they offer to demons and not to God. I do not want you to be partners with demons. [21] You cannot drink the cup of the Lord and the cup of demons. You cannot partake of the table of the Lord and the table of demons. [22] Shall we provoke the Lord to jealousy? Are we stronger than he?

Have you ever noticed how couples who have been married a long time can begin to look alike? It is a natural desire for a lover to cherish characteristics in his or her beloved and want to become more like what they see and love in the object of their affection. As followers of Jesus, we may wonder how it is that we begin to resemble him whom we love.

Paul answers this question by pointing his readers to the Eucharist: "The cup of blessing which we bless, is it not a sharing in the blood of Christ? The bread which we break, is it not a participation in the body of Christ?" (1 Corinthians 10:16). God wants to use our celebration of Mass to transform us into the image and likeness of Christ. For Paul, and for the whole early church, receiving the Eucharist meant nothing less than participating in the very life of Christ. That's why the Corinthians had to get rid of the idol worship that was part of their former lives. There was no room for such false worship if they wanted to experience the kind of transformation that was available to them in Christian worship.

Every one of us wants to see our old lives of sin die so we can grow closer to Jesus, but so many things can get in our way: busy schedules, guilt over past struggles or temptations, a longstanding grudge against a family or church member. We may even feel that neither God nor the church has any right interfering in certain parts of our lives. All these attitudes can keep us from being united with Jesus, blocking the transforming power he longs to pour out on us.

As we choose to participate in the life of Christ and put aside our reliance on the "idols" of our age, all the gifts that Jesus promised will come to life in us. We will begin to take on his character. Isn't it encouraging to know that the grace of God in the Eucharist can release us from sin, fear, and condemnation? Isn't it encouraging to know that the closer we draw to Jesus at Mass—the more deeply we partake of his life—the more we will be set free? By participating in the Eucharist with open hearts, we give God and the world an outward sign of an inner reality—our own death and resurrection with Christ.

Jesus invites us to be transformed by the "real food" of his body and blood. Let us not keep him waiting at the banquet table! Let's ask him to teach us how to worship him in Spirit and truth.

"Lord Jesus, you are my beloved, and I want to resemble you. Teach me to participate in your life more deeply, especially through the Eucharist. I want nothing more than to receive your divine life."

1 Corinthians 10:23–11:1

[23] "All things are lawful," but not all things are helpful. "All things are lawful," but not all things build up. [24] Let no one seek his own good, but the good of his neighbor. [25] Eat whatever is sold in the meat market without raising any question on the ground of conscience. [26] For "the earth is the Lord's, and everything in it." [27] If one of the unbelievers invites you to dinner and you are disposed to go, eat whatever is set before you without raising any question on the ground of conscience. [28] (But if some one says to you, "This has been offered in sacrifice," then out of consideration for the man who informed you, and for conscience' sake — [29] I mean his conscience, not yours — do not eat it.) For why should my liberty be determined by another man's scruples? [30] If I partake with thankfulness, why am I denounced because of that for which I give thanks?

[31] So, whether you eat or drink, or whatever you do, do all to the glory of God. [32] Give no offense to Jews or to Greeks or to the church of God, [33] just as I try to please all men in everything I do, not seeking my own advantage, but that of many, that they may be saved.

[1] Be imitators of me, as I am of Christ.

Let no one seek his own good, but the good of his neighbor.
(1 Corinthians 10:24)

What is freedom? A life unbounded by restrictions or rules, able to pursue whatever we desire? Do we see ourselves sipping exotic drinks on a tropical island, or dancing with joy atop a brilliant, green mountain? How many of us would choose Paul's statement as the essence of the meaning of freedom?

The Corinthians valued their personal freedom highly. Their definition, however, went something like this: "If my conscience doesn't bother me, I should be able to do it." Sounds familiar, does it not? Modern society tends to see freedom as the right to do what we want when we want, without regard to the needs or desires of others. But true freedom—the freedom Jesus came to give us—involves the "right" to be a slave to other people in love, the "right" to bring blessings to and to build up the body of Christ. True freedom, as Paul put it, involves the "right" to seek the advantage of others before ourselves.

While a worldly idea of freedom enthrones self, Christian freedom at its heart is liberation from the tyranny of self. No longer bound to sin and selfishness, we are free to choose to put others first, to put aside our own preferences or time lines for how things should work. And the wonder of Christian freedom is the way it grows in our hearts: As we give up our self-centered philosophies and live to serve others, we are set free more and more to live as Jesus lived, and to love as he loved. As we give of ourselves, we begin to resemble Jesus more and more.

Of course, this is a very countercultural position. In an age as individualistic as ours, we are bombarded with messages that urge us to guard our personal freedom at all costs. For the most part, we can come and go as we please; we have the power to choose what to wear or eat, or where to live. The idea that anyone would give up dearly held rights or inconvenience himself or herself for another is unthinkable. But the gospel is not primarily about preserving our personal freedom. It's about dying to our old lives so that the life of Christ—a life centered upon self-emptying love—can take over. Imagine the witness Christians can be in the world as we live in this freedom!

"Lord, make me truly free! Let me live by the law of love, so that all my thoughts, words, and deeds will flow from a genuine love for your people. Make me like you so that I can show the world your freedom."

Christian Worship

1 CORINTHIANS 11:2–14:40

1 Corinthians 11:2-16

[2] I commend you because you remember me in everything and maintain the traditions even as I have delivered them to you. [3] But I want you to understand that the head of every man is Christ, the head of a woman is her husband, and the head of Christ is God. [4] Any man who prays or prophesies with his head covered dishonors his head, [5] but any woman who prays or prophesies with her head unveiled dishonors her head — it is the same as if her head were shaven. [6] For if a woman will not veil herself, then she should cut off her hair; but if it is disgraceful for a woman to be shorn or shaven, let her wear a veil. [7] For a man ought not to cover his head, since he is the image and glory of God; but woman is the glory of man. [8] (For man was not made from woman, but woman from man. [9] Neither was man created for woman, but woman for man.) [10] That is why a woman ought to have a veil on her head, because of the angels. [11] (Nevertheless, in the Lord woman is not independent of man nor man of woman; [12] for as woman was made from man, so man is now born of woman. And all things are from God.) [13] Judge for yourselves; is it proper for a woman to pray to God with her head uncovered? [14] Does not nature itself teach you that for a man to wear long hair is degrading to him, [15] but if a woman has long hair, it is her pride? For her hair is given to her for a covering. [16] If any one is disposed to be contentious, we recognize no other practice, nor do the churches of God.

What did Paul mean by all this discussion about women and men and their roles in the church? It's hard for us modern readers to uncover Paul's points, and contemporary issues such as equality for women only seem to cloud the picture more. We may think Paul was rigidly advocating the subordination of women, but in truth, he was concerned about healthy relationships between men and women. Paul did not say that women could not participate in the life of the church. In fact, he himself says that they were praying and prophesying. No, Paul was focusing on a behavioral issue in the Corinthian church that was causing problems mostly because of the cultural norms of the time.

The heart of the problem, manifested in the fact that some women refused to cover their heads at church, was that some of the women assumed that truly spiritual people were above sexual distinctions. Therefore, these women did not cover their heads as was the common practice of the day. It seems that for these people, having equal value was the same as being identical. If men and women had the same dignity under God, they thought, then they should be able to play the same roles in the community—they should even look alike!

Unfortunately, this attitude made the church and its members all the poorer. While the roles of men and women are not identical, both have a vital and complementary part to play in the body of Christ, without which the body cannot be whole. As Paul told the Corinthians, "In the Lord woman is not independent of man, or man independent of woman; for as woman was made from man, so man is now born of woman. And all things are from God" (1 Corinthians 11:11-12).

What is Paul saying to us today? It has less to do with whether women cover their heads and more to do with whether each member in the church sees his or her role as necessary to the growth of the body of Christ. Paul is not talking about authority or hierarchy so much as relationship. In the church, men and women have admittedly different but essential roles to play. Each is incomplete without the other, and the church cannot be whole unless every member does its part. So let's ask the Lord what part he has for us in his body. There is no one else like us, and we are vital to the growth of the church!

"Heavenly Father, open my eyes to see the role you call me to play in your church. Help me to delight in the tasks that you have given me. I want to be a blessing and asset to your body."

1 Corinthians 11:17-26

[17] But in the following instructions I do not commend you, because when you come together it is not for the better but for the worse. [18] For, in the first place, when you assemble as a church, I hear that there are divisions among you; and I partly believe it, [19] for there must be factions among you in order that those who are genuine among you may be recognized. [20] When you meet together, it is not the Lord's supper that you eat. [21] For in eating, each one goes ahead with his own meal, and one is hungry and another is drunk. [22] What! Do you not have houses to eat and drink in? Or do you despise the church of God and humiliate those who have nothing? What shall I say to you? Shall I commend you in this? No, I will not.

[23] For I received from the Lord what I also delivered to you, that the Lord Jesus on the night when he was betrayed took bread, [24] and when he had given thanks, he broke it, and said, "This is my body which is for you. Do this in remembrance of me." [25] In the same way also the cup, after supper, saying, "This cup is the new covenant in

my blood. Do this, as often as you drink it, in remembrance of me." [26] For as often as you eat this bread and drink the cup, you proclaim the Lord's death until he comes.

In Paul's day, the Eucharist was part of a communal meal, which probably took place in someone's home. It was at this gathering that the divisions and factions in the Corinthian church were probably most visible. The people ate in separate groups. Those with plenty of food failed to share with those who were hungry, especially the poor. Some were even overindulging at the meal and getting drunk just before the Eucharistic celebration! How it must have hurt Jesus' heart to see his beloved children closing their hearts to one another in such ways!

Paul went to great pains in his letter to tell the Corinthians that in the Eucharist, everyone is meant to share in the one body of Jesus Christ. God wants unity, not division, to flow from this sacrament as each individual is united to Christ in one body. Not only does the Eucharist make us one in Christ, it is also a source of divine power to overcome all divisions and discord. We should examine our consciences before we approach the altar and pray earnestly for unity with all our brothers and sisters in Christ.

As they pondered the nature of the church and its intimate connection with the Eucharist, the Fathers of the Second Vatican Council sought to teach all believers about the oneness that we are called to: "As often as the sacrifice of the cross . . . is celebrated on the altar, the work of our redemption is carried out. Likewise, in the sacrament of the Eucharistic bread, the unity of believers, who form one body in Christ, is both expressed and brought about. All people are called to this union with Christ, who is the light of the world, from whom we go forth, through whom we live, and toward whom our whole life is directed" (*Dogmatic Constitution on the Church*, 3).

What a wonder! The Eucharist calls us together as one church despite our differences; it brings to light the barriers hidden in our hearts, and frees us from all causes of division. As we are united to Christ, we are empowered to love each member of his body, despite worldly obstacles.

"Heavenly Father, as we gather to celebrate our redemption in Christ, may we be united with one another. Help us to examine our hearts, to repent of any divisions, and to truly love all those who partake of your body and blood. By your Spirit, make your church one through the sacrifice of Christ, your beloved Son."

1 Corinthians 11:27-34

[27] Whoever, therefore, eats the bread or drinks the cup of the Lord in an unworthy manner will be guilty of profaning the body and blood of the Lord. [28] Let a man examine himself, and so eat of the bread and drink of the cup. [29] For any one who eats and drinks without discerning the body eats and drinks judgment upon himself. [30] That is why many of you are weak and ill, and some have died. [31] But if we judged ourselves truly, we should not be judged. [32] But when we are judged by the Lord, we are chastened so that we may not be condemned along with the world.

[33] So then, my brethren, when you come together to eat, wait for one another — [34] if any one is hungry, let him eat at home — lest

you come together to be condemned. About the other things I will give directions when I come.

For any one who eats and drinks without discerning the body eats and drinks judgment upon himself. (1 Corinthians 11:29)

Please! Not another overbearing, authoritarian statement from Paul! There are times in this letter when he seems to have gone out of his way to offend, or at least step on the toes of his brothers and sisters in Christ. He must have known that the Corinthians were trying to be faithful to the Lord. Why would he make such an unsettling proclamation?

Paul's boldness came from the love that drove him—love for Jesus and love for the men and women whom he had brought into the church. Paul was so convinced of the power of the Eucharist, so convinced that God would work wonders in hearts that were open to him, and so convinced that Jesus' real presence would make all the difference for believers, that he did not mince words. He wanted his beloved Corinthians to take hold of all the blessings that were available to them through the Eucharist, through the indwelling presence of God. Seeing them either oblivious to these blessings, or throwing them away, must have been agonizing!

We can have the same absolute conviction about the power of the Eucharist. Quoting from Vatican II, the *Catechism of the Catholic Church* calls it "the source and summit of the Christian life" (CCC, 1324). But it is so easy to allow distractions, past hurts, or guilt over past sins to rob us of the grace Jesus wants to give us at Mass. We may feel unworthy of God's generous blessings. We may doubt God's power to overcome our temptations. We may even wonder if new life is really available to us. But in the midst of our doubts and fears, the truth of God's love still stands.

As we approach the table of the Lord, let's remember that when we receive Christ at Communion, we are accepting not only his death, but his resurrection as well. We are receiving our own freedom from sin and celebrating our own birth into new life.

As we ponder Paul's teaching about the Eucharist, let's also ponder what St. John Chrysostom had to say about these verses: "Let us not slay ourselves by our irreverence, but with all awe and purity draw near to the Body of Christ; and when you see it set before you, say to yourself, 'Because of this body, I am no longer earth and ashes, no longer a prisoner, but free; because of this I hope for heaven, and to receive . . . immortal life, a portion with the angels, communion with Christ; this body, nailed and scourged, was more than death could stand against . . . . This is that same body that was pierced, stained with blood, that body, and out of which gushed the saving fountains, the one of blood, the other of water, for the world'" (*Homilies on First Corinthians*, 24.7).

1 Corinthians 12:1-3

[1] Now concerning spiritual gifts, brethren, I do not want you to be uninformed. [2] You know that when you were heathen, you were led astray to dumb idols, however you may have been moved. [3] Therefore I want you to understand that no one speaking by the Spirit of God ever says "Jesus be cursed!" and no one can say "Jesus is Lord" except by the Holy Spirit.

Paul knew the Corinthians' personal histories, the sophisticated pagan culture which surrounded them, and the popular intellectual thinking of the day. He also recognized the abundance of spiritual influences competing for their attention and belief.

Many members of this young church had once actively worshipped the idols and false gods of the Greek culture. Since most of the new believers had experienced various types of spiritual revelations and inspirations before, Paul felt it was crucial to lay out for them the key to discerning God's truth from all its counterfeits: The Spirit of God will exalt Jesus Christ; all others will not.

Because he had sought God all of his life, Paul had become aware of the existence of deceiving spirits and their mission to discredit—and ultimately destroy—the work of God. In his former efforts to serve God zealously, he himself had tortured and imprisoned Christians! However, after the Holy Spirit's blinding revelation of Christ on the road to Damascus, Paul was a changed man. This Pharisee of Pharisees no longer trusted in his personal convictions or inspirations. Now that he had experienced so deep a revelation from the Spirit, Paul had some basis for understanding and discerning his prior understanding of the ways of God. He began to put every thought to the test of the Holy Spirit and to reject any proposition or revelation that failed to glorify Jesus.

At the same time, he came to understand God's plan much more clearly, and he also began to experience Jesus in a personal way. In other words, Paul began to experience Jesus' words at the Last Supper: "When the Counselor comes, whom I shall send to you from the Father, even the Spirit of truth, who proceeds from the Father, he will bear witness to me" (John 15:26).

This is what Paul wanted to impart to the Corinthian believers: The same Spirit who moved them to faith in the risen Savior, the same Spirit whom they received at Baptism—this same Spirit wanted to lead and guide them every day. No longer would they be blown about by rival winds of doctrine. The Holy Spirit within them would reveal more and more truth about Jesus and how everything in heaven and on earth are under his Lordship—how they were meant for him as well! Any other "inspirations" or knowledge would be seen for what it was—counterfeit.

"Dear Jesus, thank you for sending the Holy Spirit to us so that we can become truly 'spiritual' people—people led by the Holy Spirit of God to know the Savior personally and do the Father's will."

1 Corinthians 12:4-11

[4] Now there are varieties of gifts, but the same Spirit; [5] and there are varieties of service, but the same Lord; [6] and there are varieties of working, but it is the same God who inspires them all in every one. [7] To each is given the manifestation of the Spirit for the common good. [8] To one is given through the Spirit the utterance of wisdom, and to another the utterance of knowledge according to the same Spirit, [9] to another faith by the same Spirit, to another gifts of healing by the one Spirit, [10] to another the working of miracles, to another prophecy, to another the ability to distinguish between spirits, to another various kinds of tongues, to another the interpretation of tongues. [11] All these are inspired by one and the same Spirit, who apportions to each one individually as he wills.

Have you ever been tempted to think that God created all of us, plopped us down on the earth, and then said, "Good luck! I hope you make it. I'll see you at my second coming!" Fortunately for us, nothing could be further from the truth. Rather than leaving us to survive by our wits alone, God has given us every good gift necessary to live in peace with ourselves and with each other.

God's greatest gift, of course, was his Son, Jesus. But after Jesus rose from the dead and ascended into heaven, the apostles must have had to deal with feelings of inadequacy and fear for their future. As they waited and prayed together in the upper room, God fulfilled his promise not to leave his people as orphans. He sent his Holy Spirit into their hearts as a real, discernible presence within them.

The infilling of the apostles on the day of Pentecost signified a new day for all men and women: God would take up residence within each and every one of his children and work in their hearts to transform them into his own image and likeness. Individually, each believer's body would become a holy temple, and corporately, all believers together would make up the body of Christ, the church.

God knew that as individuals, we would never be able to live up to his call to holiness. It was his plan to make us interdependent, humble, and complementary. That's why he has given each of us different gifts from the Holy Spirit. Some are for our own personal growth, but many others are for the growth of the body of Christ.

What gift is God giving you to share with others? What gift do you need to receive from someone else? All are from him, and all are important for the kingdom: speaking words of inspired wisdom, knowledge, or prophecy; demonstrating faith or gifts of healing; miracles; discerning evil from good; and even speaking and interpreting heavenly languages.

Even more "natural" gifts like hospitality, service, and administration can manifest the love and power of God. God wants to give us these gifts so that we can help people in our neighborhoods, at home, and in our churches. For instance, life and death were not at stake at the wedding feast at Cana, but Mary's concern for her host brought about Jesus' first miracle.

When a friend shares about a difficult situation, ask the Spirit to give you words of comfort or wisdom. How can God answer a prayer that is never uttered? Befriend a neighbor who is suffering—serve him or her in some tangible way and promise to pray for the Lord's comfort. Join with others who share your faith and pray regularly for your friends and neighbors. Expect God to work with you and make you an instrument of his gospel. As you do, the Lord will show you how commonplace his miracles can be in your walk with him.

"Holy Spirit, thank you for your many good gifts. Thank you for showing me how much I need my brothers and sisters on earth and how much they need me. Teach us all to share what you have given us to build one another up and to transform the church."

1 Corinthians 12:12-26

[12] For just as the body is one and has many members, and all the members of the body, though many, are one body, so it is with Christ. [13] For by one Spirit we were all baptized into one body — Jews or Greeks, slaves or free — and all were made to drink of one Spirit. [14] For the body does not consist of one member but of many. [15] If the foot should say, "Because I am not a hand, I do not belong to the body," that would not make it any less a part of the body. [16] And if the ear should say, "Because I am not an eye, I do not belong to the body," that would not make it any less a part of the body. [17] If the

whole body were an eye, where would be the hearing? If the whole body were an ear, where would be the sense of smell? [18] But as it is, God arranged the organs in the body, each one of them, as he chose. [19] If all were a single organ, where would the body be? [20] As it is, there are many parts, yet one body. [21] The eye cannot say to the hand, "I have no need of you," nor again the head to the feet, "I have no need of you." [22] On the contrary, the parts of the body which seem to be weaker are indispensable, [23] and those parts of the body which we think less honorable we invest with the greater honor, and our unpresentable parts are treated with greater modesty, [24] which our more presentable parts do not require. But God has so composed the body, giving the greater honor to the inferior part, [25] that there may be no discord in the body, but that the members may have the same care for one another. [26] If one member suffers, all suffer together; if one member is honored, all rejoice together.

Do you find yourself thinking that some Christians are more important than others? Do you catch yourself putting priests or bishops or other visible church workers on a spiritual pedestal, while downplaying the value of those seated in the pews around you? It can be very easy to view others from such a "natural" point of view. Paul, however, urges us to take another look so that we might be able to appreciate each other better.

As baptized Christians, we are all members of Christ's body and partakers in his Spirit. Nationality, gender, occupation, wealth, success—none of this has any bearing on our status in the kingdom of God. The cross of Christ is the great leveler of all time. Before it come kings and peasants, CEOs and day laborers, all equal in need, and all equal in hope. Regardless of who we are "in the world," in Christ we all have the opportunity to be sons and daughters of the King of kings! And because of our shared, exalted status, we also become brothers and sisters to each other: equal in dignity, yet differing in roles and responsibilities. In short, we are the body of Christ.

Any good biologist will tell you how important is the diversity and balance in the human body. We have only two eyes and just one heart, but millions of blood cells. This is the way it's supposed to be. Would it really be an improvement to have four hands or twelve toes? No. God has arranged everything in such a way that every part of our bodies—every major organ as well as every tiny neuron—is indispensable to the efficient functioning of the whole.

So ask yourself, "Am I important to God for the health of his body?" Yes, and so is your neighbor two doors down, and so is the young child being born on the other side of the world right now. All God's children were created for a specific purpose. When each one lives for this purpose, God's plans are easily fulfilled. When we begin to appraise some people as irrelevant and others as vitally critical, we have lost God's viewpoint. Remember: In the human body, God has given "greater honor to the inferior part, that there may be no discord in the body, but that the members may have the same care for one another. If one member suffers, all suffer together; if one member is honored, all rejoice together" (1 Corinthians 12:24-26). This is how closely connected we are in God's eyes!

"Lord Jesus, in your infinite wisdom you have made us all to be indispensable members of your body. Give us wisdom to view ourselves and others in this way so that we might learn to function smoothly together and accomplish all that your heart desires."

1 Corinthians 12:27-31

[27] Now you are the body of Christ and individually members of it. [28] And God has appointed in the church first apostles, second prophets, third teachers, then workers of miracles, then healers, helpers, administrators, speakers in various kinds of tongues. [29] Are all apostles? Are all prophets? Are all teachers? Do all work miracles? [30] Do all possess gifts of healing? Do all speak with tongues? Do all interpret? [31] But earnestly desire the higher gifts. And I will show you a still more excellent way.

What an amazing truth! We have been created to be incorporated into Jesus Christ himself! Individually, Christ has made us children of God and temples of the Holy Spirit. Corporately, all of us together form a single body: His! Jesus is the head, and we are the individual parts. Think of the complexity of the human brain. This incredibly sophisticated organ is constantly responsible for coordinating and directing thousands of smaller, interdependent parts and systems throughout our body. Amazingly, this is how Christ is functioning right now with the billions of members of his spiritual body. Everything is under his direction and care. From apostles to prophets, teachers, healers, helpers, and miracle workers, each of us has a distinct role to play, and his desire is to help us discover that role—and empower us to perform it.

Do you know what part of the Body you are? Start by looking at the ways the Lord has used you in the past. Have you seen a special gift for teaching others about him? Have you had a strong desire to help others or pray for specific needs? Has God used your witness in certain situations to have an impact on someone's life? All these and more testify to your membership—and your value—in the body of Christ.

But don't just stop with the gifts that you have already seen at work in your life. Ask for more. Reach beyond your past experiences and current expectations. If God is God, and if the same Holy Spirit who raised Jesus from the dead lives in you, anything at all is possible! Could the Father use you to pray over someone and see them healed of a serious affliction? Why not? Could he use you to speak boldly to friends or coworkers about the ways he has worked in your life? Certainly. Could the Holy Spirit give you a special word that would pierce the heart of an unbeliever? Of course! Do you believe that you can participate in modern-day deeds of power for God's glory: miracles, deliverance, even the bringing down of modern Goliaths?

Jesus said we would do greater things than he did (John 14:12). Why? Because the Holy Spirit's power would now be working through thousands and millions of Spirit-filled disciples, multiplying the powerful works of God almost infinitely. Open your heart and enlarge your expectations. Cry out to God with grateful praise. Who knows? Perhaps today you will experience the joyful tongues of angels as you worship and sing out to God. Anything is possible.

"Thank you, Holy Spirit, for making me a member of Christ's body on earth. Teach me how to live by your power and see miracles every day!"

1 Corinthians 13:1-7

[1] If I speak in the tongues of men and of angels, but have not love, I am a noisy gong or a clanging cymbal. [2] And if I have prophetic powers, and understand all mysteries and all knowledge, and if I have all faith, so as to remove mountains, but have not love, I am nothing. [3] If I give away all I have, and if I deliver my body to be burned, but have not love, I gain nothing.

[4] Love is patient and kind; love is not jealous or boastful; [5] it is not arrogant or rude. Love does not insist on its own way; it is not irritable or resentful; [6] it does not rejoice at wrong, but rejoices in the right. [7] Love bears all things, believes all things, hopes all things, endures all things.

When you read this famous hymn to love, how do you react? Don't you sometimes feel that it paints a picture that you can never hope to attain? Or do you feel moved to kneel before the Lord in gratitude and awe that this is the way he loves you?

Perhaps a key to understanding this passage lies in seeing that it comes in the middle of Paul's teaching on the gifts of the Spirit. Before anything else, love is a gift freely given by God, the highest of all the spiritual gifts. Of course, love is a calling and command as well as a gift, but we should know that God is not calling us to love out of our own resources. He knows that it's impossible for us to love unconditionally. In fact, it is because we are not capable of loving as fully as he loves that he gives us his love and the grace to extend that love to our family, friends, even our enemies.

Test yourself. How deeply do you know God's love? Prayerfully read this passage again, and consider the following questions. You may want to write your answers in a journal and come back to them periodically over the next few weeks.

- Do I believe that love is a free gift from God?
- Do I believe that God's love is not something I earn, but something I receive?
- Do I believe that God's love for me is not based on how good a person I am, but that it is unconditional and unending?
- Have I experienced—and do I continue to experience—God's love in my heart?
- When I fail to love as I should, do I persevere, trusting that God is patient and will continue to help me grow in love?

There is only one way to obey the command to love, and that is to receive God's love freely into our hearts. Let us believe that the more we receive, the more we will have to give away.

"Holy Spirit, reveal the Father's love to me more deeply. Empower me to show this love to others—especially those whom I find difficult to love."

1 Corinthians 13:8-13

[8] Love never ends; as for prophecies, they will pass away; as for tongues, they will cease; as for knowledge, it will pass away. [9] For our knowledge is imperfect and our prophecy is imperfect; [10] but when the perfect comes, the imperfect will pass away. [11] When I was a child, I

spoke like a child, I thought like a child, I reasoned like a child; when I became a man, I gave up childish ways. [12] For now we see in a mirror dimly, but then face to face. Now I know in part; then I shall understand fully, even as I have been fully understood. [13] So faith, hope, love abide, these three; but the greatest of these is love.

Division, incest, neglect of the poor, abuse of spiritual gifts, pride. How sad St. Paul must have been to hear these reports about the Corinthian church! He could tell that all these elements were the result of mixing worldly philosophies with the purity of the gospel. The Corinthians thought they were spiritual and wise, but the fruit of their behavior and the rancor in their relationships showed that they were still very immature.

In essence, the Corinthians' problem was that they had lost sight of the centrality of Jesus and the love he had come to give them. So Paul's remedy was to direct this church's attention back to the love of Christ that had first touched them and led them to conversion. Without this love, Paul told them, all the extraordinary gifts they had received were worth nothing. In fact, without this love, their existence as a church would fade into nothingness, and they would end up not much different from their neighbors who didn't believe in Jesus.

According to St. Paul, love is primarily a revelation from the Lord—a powerful unveiling of God's holiness, intimacy, and power. Such a revelation is meant to purify our emotions and become the compass guiding our thoughts and actions. Experiencing God and his love is meant to teach us that no matter how intelligent or gifted we may be, all our work and talents can amount to nothing if they are not grounded in God and his love.

Paul sought to bring healing and unity back to the Corinthians by urging them to recall this love. He knew that if they could put aside all their wrangling and self-confidence just long enough to turn back to Jesus as one body, they would begin to see their situation in a new light and come together again.

Can you recall times when you felt as if you had strayed from the centrality of God's love? What were the consequences? Spend some time today reflecting on this chapter and asking the Spirit for a fresh outpouring of love from heaven. Ask him for a greater revelation of Jesus as the lover of your soul and of all creation. Fix the eyes of your heart on the one whose riches are inexhaustible and whose gifts never fail. He never tires of giving us more and more of his love!

"Holy Spirit, open my eyes. Show me God's love and create in me a deeper love for him and for all my brothers and sisters."

1 Corinthians 14:1-12

[1] Make love your aim, and earnestly desire the spiritual gifts, especially that you may prophesy. [2] For one who speaks in a tongue speaks not to men but to God; for no one understands him, but he utters mysteries in the Spirit. [3] On the other hand, he who prophesies speaks to men for their upbuilding and encouragement and consolation. [4] He who speaks in a tongue edifies himself, but he who prophesies edifies the church. [5] Now I want you all to speak in tongues, but even more to prophesy. He who prophesies is greater than he who speaks in tongues, unless some one interprets, so that the church may be edified.

[6] Now, brethren, if I come to you speaking in tongues, how shall I benefit you unless I bring you some revelation or knowledge or prophecy or teaching? [7] If even lifeless instruments, such as the flute or the harp, do not give distinct notes, how will any one know what is played? [8] And if the bugle gives an indistinct sound, who will get ready for battle? [9] So with yourselves; if you in a tongue utter speech that is not intelligible, how will any one know what is said? For you will be speaking into the air. [10] There are doubtless many different languages in the world, and none is without meaning; [11] but if I do not know the meaning of the language, I shall be a foreigner to the speaker and the speaker a foreigner to me. [12] So with yourselves; since you are eager for manifestations of the Spirit, strive to excel in building up the church.

With this exhortation, Paul returns to the subject of spiritual gifts that he began in chapter twelve. He encourages the Corinthians to "earnestly desire the spiritual gifts," especially the gift of prophecy (1 Corinthians 14:1). Why did Paul focus on prophecy? Part of the reason was to correct the Corinthians' overemphasis on the gift of tongues. Evidently, the Corinthians believed that speaking in tongues was a sign of special holiness, so when they gathered for prayer, a number of them tried to show how spiritual they were by giving messages in unknown, heavenly languages. After all, they reasoned, if they spoke in tongues, they must have special access to heaven and therefore be worthy of extra respect and honor.

Being himself intimately familiar with the gift of tongues (14:18), Paul corrects their view and urges them to look at tongues, and all the spiritual gifts, differently. They are meant to bless and build up the whole church, not improve the image of a few! While the gift of tongues has its place primarily in an individual's life, Paul saw how prophetic words of encouragement and challenge can affect an entire body of people.

As far as Paul was concerned, every Christian is capable of some form of prophecy. When we think of prophets, perhaps we recall people like Daniel, who foretold the future, or John the Baptist, who engaged in political action. These may be ways that some prophets have served the Lord, but on the most fundamental—and important—level, a prophet is one who speaks the word of God as it has been written on his or her heart. And in this respect, each of us is called to a prophetic life. As the Fathers of Vatican II taught, every baptized Christian "shares in Christ's prophetic office." Every one of us is capable of offering "a living witness to [Christ], especially by means of a life of faith and love and by offering to God a sacrifice of praise" (*Dogmatic Constitution on the Church*, 12).

How do we become prophetic? Simply by developing a deep relationship with Jesus through prayer, Scripture, and union with the church. As we allow Jesus to fill us with his love and wisdom, we will desire to share his love with those around us. We will want to tell each other what we are learning in prayer and the things God is putting on our hearts. And, even more important, we will be open to hearing such words from those around us who have proved themselves trustworthy, especially those whom God has placed in positions of authority in the church.

Every day, we face numerous opportunities to speak words of comfort and exhortation. Let's ask the Holy Spirit, who is the giver of all good gifts, to fill our hearts with God's love and to give us the heart of Christ.

Let's ask him to give us the words to speak, and the love with which to speak them. Let's ask God to teach us how to build up his people.

1 Corinthians 14:13-19

[13] Therefore, he who speaks in a tongue should pray for the power to interpret. [14] For if I pray in a tongue, my spirit prays but my mind is unfruitful. [15] What am I to do? I will pray with the spirit and I will pray with the mind also; I will sing with the spirit and I will sing with the mind also. [16] Otherwise, if you bless with the spirit, how can any one in the position of an outsider say the "Amen" to your thanksgiving when he does not know what you are saying? [17] For you may give thanks well enough, but the other man is not edified. [18] I thank God that I speak in tongues more than you all; [19] nevertheless, in church I would rather speak five words with my mind, in order to instruct others, than ten thousand words in a tongue.

Having urged the Corinthians to make love their aim in desiring the spiritual gifts, Paul continues to discuss practical issues regarding the way they conduct their gatherings. First is prayer. It seems that the Corinthians valued praying in tongues above all the other gifts God had so graciously given them. But Paul offered some clarification: "If I pray in a tongue"—by which he meant, in a language inspired by the Holy Spirit but unknown to the person praying—"my spirit prays but my mind is unfruitful" (1 Corinthians 14:14). And that was the crux of the issue: praying with the spirit (and hence not really knowing what we are praying for) versus praying with the mind (i.e., with an open heart, listening intently for God's word and movements in us).

St. Paul was not saying that one is good and the other is not. Remember, the context of this passage is desiring spiritual gifts in order to build up the church. For that purpose, Paul held that praying "with the mind" was preferable. Praying "with the spirit" is good for an individual. It edifies—builds up, instructs, and improves—the one praying. That's crucial. That's something we all need every day! But outside of ourselves, its immediate effectiveness is limited.

Praying with the mind, however, is immediately good for the entire body of Christ. For it is when we pray with our minds actively engaged that we receive understanding, wisdom, and even prophecy from the Holy Spirit. When we pray with the mind in this way, God can use us to help other people understand his plan of salvation more fully. He can teach us how to relate better with those around us. He can equip us to teach, train, admonish, and encourage each other in wisdom and insight and intelligence (Colossians 3:16).

Imagine the impact this kind of prayer can have on our parish councils, planning committees, and ministries! Even if the thought of standing in one of these assemblies and speaking on God's behalf makes you weak in the knees, you can still look to your home and family. Imagine how your children will flourish, your love will grow, and your relationships can be strengthened as you learn to pray with an active mind, open to the movements of God. This is the prayer of the saints, the love of God in Christ Jesus poured out into our minds and hearts, for the sake of his body on earth.

"Holy Spirit, teach me to pray with my mind in the way St. Paul taught the Corinthians. I want to love others and build them up in God's love, too."

1 Corinthians 14:20-25

[20] Brethren, do not be children in your thinking; be babes in evil, but in thinking be mature. [21] In the law it is written, "By men of strange tongues and by the lips of foreigners will I speak to this people, and even then they will not listen to me, says the Lord." [22] Thus, tongues are a sign not for believers but for unbelievers, while prophecy is not for unbelievers but for believers. [23] If, therefore, the whole church assembles and all speak in tongues, and outsiders or unbelievers enter, will they not say that you are mad? [24] But if all prophesy, and an unbeliever or outsider enters, he is convicted by all, he is called to account by all, [25] the secrets of his heart are disclosed; and so, falling on his face, he will worship God and declare that God is really among you.

St. Paul wanted to help the Corinthians think differently about the spiritual gifts that were so prevalent in their church. He wanted them to ask why God would pour out such unusual gifts on people. What purpose did they serve? What did God have in mind in giving these gifts? He had already answered these questions in a general way in chapter twelve: "To each is given the manifestation of the Spirit for the common good" (1 Corinthians 12:7). God had poured out these gifts for the good of the whole body of Christ. Now he applies this general principle to two specific gifts that were causing a large part of the problem: tongues and prophecy.

Paul was urging the Corinthian believers—and us as well—to think beyond themselves. From the moment God created us, his desire and intention were that each of us would "grow up" into Christ, or take on the character of Christ in our thoughts and actions. For it is in Christ that the whole body is "joined and knitted together by every ligament with which it is equipped, as each part is working properly" (Ephesians 4:16). In other words, as we become more like Christ, we are also called to build one another up in love.

Thinking this way can be difficult sometimes, as we have been conditioned to focus most of our attention on being the best individual we can be. The world tells us to strive, excel, and achieve individually, even sometimes at the expense of other people. But God says that it is by serving one another that we will truly reach our fullest potential, which is nothing less than the fullness of Christ himself. And so, the gifts of the Spirit—whichever gifts God has bestowed upon each of us—are meant to be the tools we use for crafting the body of Christ into the form our Father desires.

God wants our faith to be the kind that draws other people to Christ. Paul exhorted the Corinthians to think about who was in their assemblies before they began prophesying or speaking in tongues, so that unbelievers might understand what they were saying and so come to worship God themselves (1 Corinthians 14:25). Isn't that what we want, too? Not just in church, but in our families, neighborhoods, workplaces, and schools?

St. John Chrysostom declared, "As it is the [builder's] work to build, so it is the Christian's to profit his neighbors in all things" (*Homilies on First Corinthians*, 36.4). No wonder God bestows amazing gifts on us: We have an amazing calling. Let's not keep these gifts for ourselves, but be mature in our thinking as we go out to serve the people of the world.

"Jesus, thank you for calling me to be in your body. Expand my thinking about how and why I serve you, so that I might grow in maturity and build up your church."

1 Corinthians 14:26-33a

[26] What then, brethren? When you come together, each one has a hymn, a lesson, a revelation, a tongue, or an interpretation. Let all things be done for edification. [27] If any speak in a tongue, let there be only two or at most three, and each in turn; and let one interpret. [28] But if there is no one to interpret, let each of them keep silence in church and speak to himself and to God. [29] Let two or three prophets speak, and let the others weigh what is said. [30] If a revelation is made to another sitting by, let the first be silent. [31] For you can all prophesy one by one, so that all may learn and all be encouraged; [32] and the spirits of prophets are subject to prophets. [33] For God is not a God of confusion but of peace.

Having encouraged the Corinthians to reach out to other people, especially those who were not Christians, Paul moved on to remind them that they are also to serve and edify one another when they gather for worship. "Each one," he wrote, should come with "a hymn, a lesson, a revelation" and so on (1 Corinthians 14:26). Every member of the church should take responsibility for the gatherings of prayer and ask how they can contribute to the edification of everyone present. According to St. John Chrysostom, this was not just a good idea. It was "the foundation and the rule of Christianity" (*Homilies on First Corinthians*, 36.4).

Wouldn't it be amazing if our love for one another, our prayer together, our reading and studying Scripture together, or our celebration of the Eucharist together struck someone to the heart to such an extent that he or she fell prostrate and began worshipping God? Or how about applying the same thinking outside of Mass? Most of us see some of the same people every day: family members, coworkers, neighbors, store clerks, and so on. How would the lives of those around us change if we were to pray every morning for each person we know we will see that day?

The possibilities are as limitless as the power of God! We have only to ask, and the Holy Spirit will give us a word—perhaps of encouragement for one who is discouraged, or of wisdom for someone struggling with a difficult situation. The Holy Spirit can give us understanding, counsel, discernment, healing, and, most importantly, God's own love to share with those around us. In other words, we too can live as the prophetic people Paul described in this passage.

We become prophetic not necessarily by telling the future, or declaring the mind of God to someone—although those things might happen if we ask. No, we become prophetic by loving others and seeking to do all things "for edification" (14:26); by asking God to give us words of encouragement and humble exhortation for the people in our lives. The love of God, poured out in our hearts and overflowing to others—to believers and unbelievers alike—will ground us in our faith and enable us to live prophetically.

"Holy Spirit, make me know God's ways and teach me, that I might build your body today. Let your love overflow from me in words and actions that will build up and strengthen all whom I meet."

1 Corinthians 14:33b-40

[33] As in all the churches of the saints, [34] the women should keep silence in the churches. For they are not permitted to speak, but should be subordinate, as even the law says. [35] If there is anything they desire to know, let them ask their husbands at home. For it is shameful for a woman to speak in church. [36] What! Did the word of God originate with you, or are you the only ones it has reached? [37] If any one thinks that he is a prophet, or spiritual, he should acknowledge that what I am writing to you is a command of the Lord. [38] If any one does not recognize this, he is not recognized. [39] So, my brethren, earnestly desire to prophesy, and do not forbid speaking in tongues; [40] but all things should be done decently and in order.

What a lot of trouble this passage can cause these days! Was Paul really a chauvinistic woman-hater? Hardly! Remember how he started out this chapter: "Make love your aim" (1 Corinthians 14:1). He wouldn't tolerate arguments about which spiritual gift was "better," nor did he have time for infighting about the place of women in worship. To focus all our attention on these kinds of arguments only keeps alive the very differences Paul was trying to put to rest!

"Did the word of God originate with you," he asks the men, "Are you the only ones it has reached?" (1 Corinthians 14:36). The answer, of course, is a resounding no. We can almost hear him urge, "So move on! Look to the things you agree on, and in everything else, make love your aim. Those who speak in tongues should love the prophets; the men should respect the women; and everyone should strive to edify their brothers and sisters in Christ. That's the only way your church can be healed of divisions and grow in holiness."

Brothers and sisters, we are called to love and respect our fellow believers. No one of us is the sole repository of God's word. God has brought us all together as a church for one simple reason: We need each other! "For the body does not consist of one member but of many. . . . God has so composed the body . . . that there may be no discord in the body, but that the members may have the same care for one another" (1 Corinthians 12:14,24-25). We should move away from arguments about gifts and positions and the like, and make love our aim!

Let us, then, love all believers in Jesus Christ. "Let us love one another, for love is of God, and he who loves is born of God and knows God" (1 John 4:7). Our love for one another—despite our differences, both within the Catholic Church and between other denominations—is a witness to the world of the power and love of God. Let us rid ourselves of judgments and biases. Yes, let us make love our aim. As we do, unity of heart and mind will surely follow.

"Father, purify my heart. Clean out the litter of prejudice and judgment, and replace it with your love. Teach me to love others as you love me. Make my life one that respects and encourages my fellow believers, so that your church can become an even brighter light shining in a darkened world."

The Resurrection

1 Corinthians 15–16

1 Corinthians 15:1-11

[1] Now I would remind you, brethren, in what terms I preached to you the gospel, which you received, in which you stand, [2] by which you are saved, if you hold it fast — unless you believed in vain.
[3] For I delivered to you as of first importance what I also received, that Christ died for our sins in accordance with the scriptures, [4] that he was buried, that he was raised on the third day in accordance with the scriptures, [5] and that he appeared to Cephas, then to the twelve. [6] Then he appeared to more than five hundred brethren at one time, most of whom are still alive, though some have fallen asleep. [7] Then he appeared to James, then to all the apostles. [8] Last of all, as to one untimely born, he appeared also to me. [9] For I am the least of the apostles, unfit to be called an apostle, because I persecuted the church of God. [10] But by the grace of God I am what I am, and his grace toward me was not in vain. On the contrary, I worked harder than any of them, though it was not I, but the grace of God which is with me. [11] Whether then it was I or they, so we preach and so you believed.

As he encouraged the Corinthian Christians toward maturity and unity, Paul cited an early profession of faith that they may well have proclaimed when they gathered to celebrate the Eucharist: "That Christ died for our sins in accordance with the scriptures, that he was buried, that he was raised on the third day in accordance with the scriptures" (1 Corinthians 15:3-4). This affirmation was based on the reports of eyewitnesses: "He appeared to Cephas, then to the twelve. Then he appeared to more than five hundred brethren . . . to James, then to all the apostles" (15:5-7).

Paul knew that this core belief could unite the Corinthians despite their many differences of opinion. He also knew that this creed linked them with the larger church spread throughout the world. The struggling believers at Corinth were brothers and sisters with James, Peter (Cephas), and the other apostles. They were related to all those who had seen the Lord, but who—like them—faced serious obstacles to their faith. Peter, for instance, had denied the Lord three times (Mark 14:72); James and John asked Jesus for places of honor (10:37); Mary Magdalene fled in fear and confusion at the resurrection (16:8); Thomas doubted that Jesus was risen (John 20:25).

These witnesses of the risen Lord were not superheroes but real human beings who cooperated with God's Spirit. In overcoming their weaknesses, they echoed Paul's confession, "It was not I, but the grace of God which is with me" (1 Corinthians 15:10). No one was better than anyone else. All were weak and sinful; all had been redeemed by the blood of Christ.

We are all called to become builders of the church. No one is excluded from the privilege—or the demands—of living as a witness for Christ. God's gifts are not meant to stay hidden. What about you? Can you testify to a healing in your family? Do you experience joy at Mass, in receiving the sacraments, in personal prayer? We can touch many lives as we "recount the deeds of the LORD" (Psalm 118:17).

"We believe in you, risen Savior! Enlarge our ability to pass along what you have given to us. Guide us in proclaiming your great deeds in our midst."

1 Corinthians 15:12-19

[12] Now if Christ is preached as raised from the dead, how can some of you say that there is no resurrection of the dead? [13] But if there is no resurrection of the dead, then Christ has not been raised; [14] if Christ has not been raised, then our preaching is in vain and your faith is in vain. [15] We are even found to be misrepresenting God, because we testified of God that he raised Christ, whom he did not raise if it is true that the dead are not raised. [16] For if the dead are not raised, then Christ has not been raised. [17] If Christ has not been raised, your faith is futile and you are still in your sins. [18] Then those also who have fallen asleep in Christ have perished. [19] If for this life only we have hoped in Christ, we are of all men most to be pitied.

The Corinthians had become so caught up in the wrangling and infighting in their church that they lost sight of the power and wonder of the gospel. Controversies over leadership, the gifts of the Spirit, obedience to the commands of the Lord, even civil lawsuits clouded their vision and lowered their expectations. It got to the point that some even began to discount God's promise to raise us up at the second coming and give us glorified bodies. How easy it can be to lose sight of our inheritance in Christ! How quickly cares and concerns can cloud our vision!

God's plan for us is that our faith—grounded in Jesus' death and resurrection—will continue to grow and become increasingly expansive. He wants to open our eyes to see his love and his promises more clearly every day. There is no limit to what he can do in those who rely on him. Imagine how different life would be if we could trust that Jesus is able to do for us, today, all the things we read about him doing when he walked the earth two thousand years ago!

Take Mary Magdalene as an example. She probably did not start following Jesus expecting to experience everything that happened to her. She probably would have been happy just with the forgiveness and deliverance she knew at first (Luke 8:2). But that wasn't enough for Jesus. He allowed her to be the first witness of his resurrection and made her the bearer of the gospel to the apostles! Because she clung to Jesus, she ended up receiving far more than she had ever imagined.

The same can happen for us today. How big is your vision of the gospel? Does it include healings? Miracles? New beginnings? Release from age-old burdens? Does it include the promise of a bodily resurrection? The Corinthians had lost sight of the bigness of the gospel. Have we? The only real antidote to this is to let the Holy Spirit impress upon us continually how gloriously encompassing the gospel is. Let's ask the Spirit to increase our vision and expectancy.

"Holy Spirit, help me to know the power of the gospel more fully. Open my eyes to see beyond my limited scope so that I can experience the wonder of your life in me today!"

1 Corinthians 15:20-29

[20] But in fact Christ has been raised from the dead, the first fruits of those who have fallen asleep. [21] For as by a man came death, by a man has come also the resurrection of the dead. [22] For as in Adam all die, so also in Christ shall all be made alive. [23] But each in his own order: Christ the first fruits, then at his coming those who belong to

Christ. [24] Then comes the end, when he delivers the kingdom to God the Father after destroying every rule and every authority and power. [25] For he must reign until he has put all his enemies under his feet. [26] The last enemy to be destroyed is death. [27] "For God has put all things in subjection under his feet." But when it says, "All things are put in subjection under him," it is plain that he is excepted who put all things under him. [28] When all things are subjected to him, then the Son himself will also be subjected to him who put all things under him, that God may be everything to every one.

[29] Otherwise, what do people mean by being baptized on behalf of the dead? If the dead are not raised at all, why are people baptized on their behalf?

The fact that the church has included a day like All Souls Day in its liturgical calendar is a powerful testimony to the fact that every Christian shares in Jesus' victory over death. The fact that we will one day join the company of "all souls"—those who have died—should not make us feel fear, since we know, in faith, that "as in Adam all die, so also in Christ shall all be made alive" (1 Corinthians 15:22).

God has not left us to wander aimlessly in this world, without hope or purpose. He created us for a purpose far greater than what we typically assume in the confines of our earthly existence. Not only will we live again; at the end of time, we will see the full revelation of the Father's glory. Although our redemption has already been accomplished on the cross, on that great day when Jesus "delivers the kingdom to God the Father," his victory will be fully revealed (1 Corinthians 15:24). Sin, suffering, and death itself—"the last enemy"—will be destroyed (15:26). Everything that troubles, confuses, or tempts us now will be wiped away, "that God may be everything to every one" (15:28).

Even now, as we long for the fulfillment of God's plan, we can be filled with the hope of a life of complete joy in God's presence. It is this hope that gives us confidence to pray for the dead, just as Christians have done since earliest times. Trusting in God's mercy, we pray that those who have died in their imperfections may be purified more deeply and made ready to meet the Bridegroom—to see God face to face.

St. Cyril of Jerusalem (*c.* 315-386) witnessed to this tradition of praying for the dead, especially during the celebration of the Eucharist: "We pray for the holy bishops and fathers who have fallen asleep ahead of us, and we pray in their behalf, while here in the presence of the holy and awesome victim" (*Mystagogical Cathecheses*, 5:9). This kind of intercession for one another is possible because of our union with all those who belong to Christ, a union that is not broken—even by death.

Let us pray that as we ponder our inheritance in Christ, our minds will be lifted beyond the boundaries of this life, and that we may be living witnesses to those around us.

1 Corinthians 15:30-34

[30] Why am I in peril every hour? [31] I protest, brethren, by my pride in you which I have in Christ Jesus our Lord, I die every day! [32] What do I gain if, humanly speaking, I fought with beasts at Ephesus? If the dead are not raised, "Let us eat and drink, for tomorrow we die."
[33] Do not be deceived: "Bad company ruins good morals." [34] Come to your right mind, and sin no more. For some have no knowledge of God. I say this to your shame.

It's often been said that Christianity without the resurrection is not simply Christianity without its final chapter—it's not Christianity at all! Christ's resurrection has the greatest implications of anything that has ever happened in the history of humankind—and those implications extend from the first Easter morning to our present day and beyond, through all eternity. Not only have we been redeemed from our sin through Jesus' death and resurrection, we mortal humans are offered immortality. Our bodies will be raised from the decay of death and we will see Jesus and the Father with physical eyes! We will live eternally in paradise, inheriting "a new heaven and a new earth" (Revelation 21:1) that far surpasses the beauty of any imagined Eden!

Yet some of the Corinthians said there is no resurrection of the dead (1 Corinthians 15:12). After staunchly defending the truth of the resurrection—both Christ's and that of those who have died—Paul scoffed at the faulty reasoning of those who seemed to have even thought, since there is no life after death, that they might as well live just as they pleased (15:32). "Don't be deceived into living immorally," he cautioned them. "Remember God, come to your senses, and stop sinning!" (15:33-34).

Like the Corinthians, we, too, risk the eternal consequences of living carelessly. In words that echo Paul's, St. Alphonsus Liguori, a revered eighteenth-century spiritual director and founder of the Redemptorists, urged all Christians to put aside sin and live righteously, keeping their future immortality in mind:

> What would it profit you to be happy here (if it were possible for a soul to be happy without God), if after this you must be miserable for all eternity? . . . Is he not a fool who seeks after happiness in this world, where he will remain only a few days,

> and exposes himself to the risk of being unhappy in the next, where he must live for eternity?
>
> Dearly beloved Christians, if you were to die and your fate for eternity was to be decided before nightfall, would you be ready? . . . Then why don't you, now that God gives you this time, settle the accounts of your conscience? Do you think, perhaps, that it cannot happen that this will be the last day for you? . . . My brother, to save your soul you must give up sin. (St. Alphonsus Liguori, *Preparation for Death*)

"Heavenly Father, may the hope of the resurrection give me courage and joy in pressing on toward the goal for the prize of your upward call in Christ Jesus (Philippians 3:14). Help me to put aside sin and live according to your ways so that I may one day come to see you face to face!"

1 Corinthians 15:35-49

[35] But some one will ask, "How are the dead raised? With what kind of body do they come?" [36] You foolish man! What you sow does not come to life unless it dies. [37] And what you sow is not the body which is to be, but a bare kernel, perhaps of wheat or of some other grain. [38] But God gives it a body as he has chosen, and to each kind of seed its own body. [39] For not all flesh is alike, but there is one kind for men, another for animals, another for birds, and another for fish. [40] There are celestial bodies and there are terrestrial bodies; but the glory of the

celestial is one, and the glory of the terrestrial is another. [41] There is one glory of the sun, and another glory of the moon, and another glory of the stars; for star differs from star in glory.

[42] So is it with the resurrection of the dead. What is sown is perishable, what is raised is imperishable. [43] It is sown in dishonor, it is raised in glory. It is sown in weakness, it is raised in power. [44] It is sown a physical body, it is raised a spiritual body. If there is a physical body, there is also a spiritual body. [45] Thus it is written, "The first man Adam became a living being"; the last Adam became a life-giving spirit. [46] But it is not the spiritual which is first but the physical, and then the spiritual. [47] The first man was from the earth, a man of dust; the second man is from heaven. [48] As was the man of dust, so are those who are of the dust; and as is the man of heaven, so are those who are of heaven. [49] Just as we have borne the image of the man of dust, we shall also bear the image of the man of heaven.

A ghost stood at heaven's edge with a hideous red lizard perched on his shoulder. The lizard, whiplike tail twitching, whispered unseemly suggestions in the ghost's ear. Presently the ghost smiled and turned to walk away. At that moment, a flaming angel stopped him and offered to kill the lizard for him so that he could enter heaven. The ghost agreed initially, then backed away. He feared that he could not live without this lizard. Sure it was painful at times, but he had become used to it. Besides, he said, the lizard also gave him pleasures he couldn't imagine living without.

When the angel explained that he couldn't enter heaven with the lizard, the ghost wavered somewhat, but held firm. It took all the angel had to convince the ghost that he really would be better off without this hideous creature digging into his shoulder. Eventually, he consented, and the angel seized the lizard and hurled it to the ground. The ghost cried out in agony at first, but then, freed from his affliction, he was gloriously transformed and, radiant and joyful, charged into heaven to meet the Lord.

This allegory, from C. S. Lewis' book *The Great Divorce*, is an excellent illustration of St. Paul's words to the Corinthians. Our natural lives are only a kernel of what God intends for us. God's desire is to raise us up to the full glory for which we were created, but this resurrection only comes through the death of our old lives of sin.

Jesus himself said, "unless a grain of wheat . . . dies, it remains alone; but if it dies, it bears much fruit" (John 12:24). Every day, he calls us to yield our lives to the cross so that he can put to death whatever is opposed to him. As we do, we will be raised up to a glorious new life. We will experience the power of his resurrection in increasing measure!

Like the ghost, we too strive for self-preservation. We even try to preserve those aspects of our lives that are far from glorious. But there is hope at the cross. What dies there is perishable, but what is raised is imperishable.

Jesus wants to transform you. Let him put to death those things in your nature that hinder you from knowing and receiving God's love. As you do, the new life you will receive will far surpass your old life as your relationship with Jesus takes on increasingly glorious dimensions.

"Lord, you know me intimately. All my thoughts, words, and ways are plain to you. As your right hand holds me and leads me to your cross, help me to die a little more to myself so that your life in me can increase."

1 Corinthians 15:50-58

[50] I tell you this, brethren: flesh and blood cannot inherit the kingdom of God, nor does the perishable inherit the imperishable.
[51] Lo! I tell you a mystery. We shall not all sleep, but we shall all be changed, [52] in a moment, in the twinkling of an eye, at the last trumpet. For the trumpet will sound, and the dead will be raised imperishable, and we shall be changed. [53] For this perishable nature must put on the imperishable, and this mortal nature must put on immortality. [54] When the perishable puts on the imperishable, and the mortal puts on immortality, then shall come to pass the saying that is written:

> "Death is swallowed up in victory."
> [55] "O death, where is thy victory?
> O death, where is thy sting?"

[56] The sting of death is sin, and the power of sin is the law. [57] But thanks be to God, who gives us the victory through our Lord Jesus Christ.
[58] Therefore, my beloved brethren, be steadfast, immovable, always abounding in the work of the Lord, knowing that in the Lord your labor is not in vain.

Paul brings his lengthy discourse about the resurrection to an end with a jubilant cry of triumph. We can almost hear him exultantly thundering at us from the page as we read his words—"Thanks be to God, who gives us the victory through our Lord Jesus Christ!" (1 Corinthians 15:57).

Centuries earlier, the prophet Hosea had portrayed God as a passionate lover pursuing Israel, and had asked whether God, grieved by his chosen people's repeated faithlessness, should deliver them from death (Hosea 13:14-16). Hosea's verses implied that the answer was no, as God summoned the stings and plagues of death to chastise his people. Was there to be no hope or rescue?

Indeed, as sinners, we deserved to die. Our first parents had disobeyed God, and sin—death's destructive "sting"—infected humankind with a fatal poison. Without the hope of eternal life, with a view of human life limited to the present only, the specter of death overshadowed us. Our way of thinking and how we approached every aspect of our lives—our personal relationships, our possessions, our goals—were shaped by our mortality. Yet Paul's pen could give Hosea's stinging, bitter words a new shade of meaning in light of Christ's death and resurrection. God had mercy on us! Jesus Christ redeemed us from sin and broke the stranglehold death had on us! Since Christ had overcome death—"swallowed it up" (1 Corinthians 15:54)—Paul could cry in triumph, "O death, where is your sting?" (15:55). Now our perishable human nature can put on the imperishable, our mortal nature immortality (15:54).

Jesus has drawn out the poison from death, and its bite is no longer eternally fatal. We are not of this earth only! We have a higher horizon. We have all the blessings of heaven, all the power of the Spirit's ministry, to sustain us and to lift us above the limited expectations of this present world. May we, then, abound in the work of the Lord, knowing that in him none of our present efforts and labors are in vain (1 Corinthians 15:58), because we will live forever with God!

"Glory to you, Lord Jesus Christ! By your cross and resurrection, you won victory over sin and death! Thank you for inviting me to share in that victory. Thank you for giving me the hope of being with you for all eternity!"

1 Corinthians 16:1-14

[1] Now concerning the contribution for the saints: as I directed the churches of Galatia, so you also are to do. [2] On the first day of every week, each of you is to put something aside and store it up, as he may prosper, so that contributions need not be made when I come. [3] And when I arrive, I will send those whom you accredit by letter to carry your gift to Jerusalem. [4] If it seems advisable that I should go also, they will accompany me.

[5] I will visit you after passing through Macedo'nia, for I intend to pass through Macedo'nia, [6] and perhaps I will stay with you or even spend the winter, so that you may speed me on my journey, wherever I go. [7] For I do not want to see you now just in passing; I hope to spend some time with you, if the Lord permits. [8] But I will stay in Ephesus until Pentecost, [9] for a wide door for effective work has opened to me, and there are many adversaries.

[10] When Timothy comes, see that you put him at ease among you, for he is doing the work of the Lord, as I am. [11] So let no one despise him. Speed him on his way in peace, that he may return to me; for I am expecting him with the brethren.

[12] As for our brother Apol'los, I strongly urged him to visit you with the other brethren, but it was not at all his will to come now. He will come when he has opportunity.

[13] Be watchful, stand firm in your faith, be courageous, be strong. [14] Let all that you do be done in love.

Let all that you do be done in love. (1 Corinthians 16:14)

What a concise yet definitive guideline for daily living! While deeply spiritual in his outlook, Paul was ever practical in how he lived out the gospel message. For example, he clearly considered feeding the hungry and contributing to the poor concrete ways of fulfilling the gospel's call to love Christ (Matthew 25:34-40; Galatians 2:10). And it was just these sorts of charitable deeds and works of mercy that he urged the Corinthians to perform with a generous dose of love.

Paul encouraged the churches he founded to take up a collection for the brothers and sisters in the Jerusalem community who were suffering from famine (1 Corinthians 16:1; Acts 11:29-30; Romans 15:25-27). He saw the contributions from the Corinthian community and other predominantly gentile Christian churches to the Jewish Christians in Jerusalem as a symbol of the unity and love of the whole church. Today, the church's universality and its solidarity of love continue to be expressed through "Peter's Pence," the pope's annual collection for the poor taken up in Catholic parishes all around the world.

Giving generously from the heart is a practical means of putting our Christian faith into action: "If a brother or sister is ill-clad and in lack of daily food, and one of you says to them, 'Go in peace, be warmed and filled,' without giving them the things needed for the body, what does it profit? So faith by itself, if it has no works, is dead" (James 2:15-17). Just as Paul appealed to the Corinthians, "On the first day of every week, each of you is to put something aside" in support of their fellow Christians (1 Corinthians 16:2), God also invites us to contribute to our parish church and support the life we share together there through the weekly Sunday collection. In addition, offering hospitality to guests, volunteering to help out in our local community, bringing a meal to a sick neighbor, and raising money to support the work of overseas missionaries are all deeds we can "do in love," opening our hearts to the world beyond the boundaries of our own parish.

"Come, Holy Spirit, and widen my heart, so that everything I do is done in love. I want to give generously of all that you have given to me."

1 Corinthians 16:15-24

[15] Now, brethren, you know that the household of Steph'anas were the first converts in Acha'ia, and they have devoted themselves to the service of the saints; [16] I urge you to be subject to such men and to every fellow worker and laborer. [17] I rejoice at the coming of Steph'anas and Fortuna'tus and Acha'icus, because they have made up for your absence; [18] for they refreshed my spirit as well as yours. Give recognition to such men.

[19] The churches of Asia send greetings. Aq'uila and Prisca, together with the church in their house, send you hearty greetings in the Lord. [20] All the brethren send greetings. Greet one another with a holy kiss.

[21] I, Paul, write this greeting with my own hand. [22] If any one has no love for the Lord, let him be accursed. Our Lord, come! [23] The grace of the Lord Jesus be with you. [24] My love be with you all in Christ Jesus. Amen.

"Farewell," the traditional English word of parting, expresses one's hopes to another that they remain in good health, in a happy state of being—literally, that one might "fare well" in life. Similarly, we send birthday and get well greeting cards to express our best wishes to another for their well-being. In each of his thirteen epistles included in the New Testament, Paul's opening salutation was a greeting wishing those he was writing to God's grace and peace. And, he unfailingly closed each of these letters in the same way he began them, repeating the blessing of grace.

Like bookends, this benediction of "grace" framed all of Paul's desires and hopes for the church in Corinth that he dearly loved and had labored to establish. He opened his epistle to them with the refrain: "Grace to you and peace from God our Father and the Lord Jesus Christ" (1 Corinthians 1:3). And though he sternly addressed problems among the Corinthians, Paul nonetheless ended his letter to them with a heartfelt expression of affection and goodwill far richer than "farewell" or "best wishes": "The grace of the Lord Jesus be with you. My love be with you all in Christ Jesus" (16:23).

Paul's tender love for the Corinthians tempered the strong admonitions and correction that he addressed to their community several times throughout his letter. His warm closing bestowed God's grace on these believers who were at once both so rich in spiritual gifts yet so torn with factions and affected by an environment rife with immorality. In addition, the many greetings Paul included at the end of this epistle from coworkers and churches throughout Asia are a sign of unity and of the love that these early Christians had for one another.

Grace—the gift of God's presence living in them—was the source of the Corinthians' spiritual well-being and strength. So it remains today for each Christian in every congregation around the world. Grace—the life of God within us—provides all that we need, whether the ability to love generously and freely, maintain peace and unity in our family and parish community, or live in faith and humility. May the grace of the Lord Jesus be with us all!

"Jesus, how great are the riches of your grace! Thank you for dwelling in me. Help me to live my life in love and gratitude to you for this great gift."

The Blessings and Pain of Christian Ministry

2 Corinthians 1–6

2 Corinthians 1:1-11

[1] Paul, an apostle of Christ Jesus by the will of God, and Timothy our brother.

To the church of God which is at Corinth, with all the saints who are in the whole of Acha'ia:

[2] Grace to you and peace from God our Father and the Lord Jesus Christ.

[3] Blessed be the God and Father of our Lord Jesus Christ, the Father of mercies and God of all comfort, [4] who comforts us in all our affliction, so that we may be able to comfort those who are in any affliction, with the comfort with which we ourselves are comforted by God. [5] For as we share abundantly in Christ's sufferings, so through Christ we share abundantly in comfort too. [6] If we are afflicted, it is for your comfort and salvation; and if we are comforted, it is for your comfort, which you experience when you patiently endure the same sufferings that we suffer. [7] Our hope for you is unshaken; for we know that as you share in our sufferings, you will also share in our comfort.

[8] For we do not want you to be ignorant, brethren, of the affliction we experienced in Asia; for we were so utterly, unbearably crushed that we despaired of life itself. [9] Why, we felt that we had received the sentence of death; but that was to make us rely not on ourselves but on God who raises the dead; [10] he delivered us from so deadly a peril, and he will deliver us; on him we have set our hope that he will deliver us again. [11] You also must help us by prayer, so that many will give thanks on our behalf for the blessing granted us in answer to many prayers.

As "an apostle of Christ Jesus by the will of God" (2 Corinthians 1:1), Paul had learned to ask how his experiences—both as a pastor and as an individual Christian—could be used to help build up the church. Thus, when writing to address problems among his brothers and sisters in Corinth, Paul had become accustomed to pointing people's eyes heavenward: "If we are afflicted, it is for your comfort and salvation; and if we are comforted, it is for your comfort" (1:6).

Paul probably composed much of 2 Corinthians around A.D. 55. However, because certain segments of the epistle appear disjointed and do not flow cohesively, many scholars theorize that the "letter" we have is a composite of more than one letter. Paul himself alluded to sending other letters, in addition to 1 Corinthians (2 Corinthians 2:4); perhaps some of these letters were edited together by one of Paul's disciples.

Despite the rather fragmented structure of 2 Corinthians, parts of the letter reflect a unifying theme—that becoming a minister of the gospel entails leaving this world behind and entering the service of Christ. Paul boasted about being an apostle (2 Corinthians 10:8; 11:5) because he knew that despite his background as an arrogant persecutor of Christians, God had mercy on him and called him into his service. In Paul's eyes, all believers can boast that they too are "ambassadors" of "the Father of mercies and God of all comfort" (5:20; 1:3).

Paul knew that God's comfort goes beyond enjoying pleasant surroundings. Through imprisonment, persecution, and even rejection by fellow believers, he learned to depend on the peace and security found only in the Lord. Speaking from experience, Paul taught that God's indwelling Spirit always "comforts us in all our affliction, so that we may be able to comfort those who are in any affliction, with the comfort with which we ourselves are comforted by God" (2 Corinthians 1:4). As we begin reading this letter, let us seek a better understanding of the comfort of God.

"Father, we rejoice in your comforting presence this day. Like your servant Paul, we claim this gift. Enable us to minister your love to others. Open our eyes to those who need your comfort, and embolden us to proclaim your Son, Jesus."

2 Corinthians 1:12-22

12 For our boast is this, the testimony of our conscience that we have behaved in the world, and still more toward you, with holiness and godly sincerity, not by earthly wisdom but by the grace of God. 13 For we write you nothing but what you can read and understand; I hope you will understand fully, 14 as you have understood in part, that you can be proud of us as we can be of you, on the day of the Lord Jesus.

15 Because I was sure of this, I wanted to come to you first, so that you might have a double pleasure; 16 I wanted to visit you on my way to Macedo'nia, and to come back to you from Macedo'nia and have you send me on my way to Judea. 17 Was I vacillating when I wanted to do this? Do I make my plans like a worldly man, ready to say Yes and No at once? 18 As surely as God is faithful, our word to you has not been Yes and No. 19 For the Son of God, Jesus Christ, whom we preached among you, Silva'nus and Timothy and I, was not Yes and No; but in him it is always Yes. 20 For all the promises of God find their Yes in him. That is why we utter the Amen through him, to the glory of God. 21 But it is God who establishes us with you in Christ, and has commissioned us; 22 he has put his seal upon us and given us his Spirit in our hearts as a guarantee.

Paul planned his second missionary journey with stops at Corinth, both on his way to Macedonia and on his return to Judea. When he decided not to make the second visit, the Corinthians questioned Paul's motives. Maybe they thought Paul was trying to avoid them, or that he had begun to consider them less important than other churches in the area. Whatever the Corinthians' reasons, Paul was hurt by their mistrust.

Paul could have responded to his brothers and sisters by justifying his change in plans, explaining in detail why he decided against a second visit. Or, he could have admonished them for their jealousy or suspicion. Instead, Paul chose to direct his readers' attention to God, who would never disappoint them, and whose guiding hand was behind everything that happened.

Paul told the Corinthians that whether or not he had been faithful to them, they could always count on God's faithfulness: "All the promises of God find their Yes in him" (2 Corinthians 1:20). God is always true to his promises; he never changes. Paul sought to assure the Corinthians that his only motivation was to love and obey God and serve them as an apostle. When faced with a difficult decision (whether to return to Corinth or not), he did not rely on his own ideas of what would be best. Rather, he did what he thought God wanted of him, and entrusted the Corinthians into his hands.

Looking beyond the problem at hand and recalling what united him with the Corinthians, Paul wrote: "It is God who established us with you in Christ. . . . He has put his seal upon us and given us his Spirit in our hearts as a guarantee" (2 Corinthians 1:21-22). Paul's confidence in God's faithfulness enabled him to glimpse more of God's glorious nature, even as he risked disappointing his friends. God assured Paul that if he obeyed, everyone involved would ultimately experience his peace, even if the path was difficult at first.

"Father, we thank you for giving us Paul's witness of what it means to surrender our lives to you. By your Spirit may we know more fully your faithfulness, so that we would have the ability to trust in you, whatever our circumstances. Father, our lives are in your hands."

2 Corinthians 1:23–2:11

[23] But I call God to witness against me — it was to spare you that I refrained from coming to Corinth. [24] Not that we lord it over your faith; we work with you for your joy, for you stand firm in your faith.

[1] For I made up my mind not to make you another painful visit. [2] For if I cause you pain, who is there to make me glad but the one whom I have pained? [3] And I wrote as I did, so that when I came I might not suffer pain from those who should have made me rejoice, for I felt sure of all of you, that my joy would be the joy of you all. [4] For I wrote you out of much affliction and anguish of heart and with many tears, not to cause you pain but to let you know the abundant love that I have for you.

[5] But if any one has caused pain, he has caused it not to me, but in some measure — not to put it too severely — to you all. [6] For such a one this punishment by the majority is enough; [7] so you should rather turn to forgive and comfort him, or he may be overwhelmed by excessive sorrow. [8] So I beg you to reaffirm your love for him. [9] For this is why I wrote, that I might test you and know whether you are obedient in everything. [10] Any one whom you forgive, I also forgive. What I have forgiven, if I have forgiven anything, has been for your sake in the presence of Christ, [11] to keep Satan from gaining the advantage over us; for we are not ignorant of his designs.

Apparently Paul was hurt by a member of the community in Corinth during one of his previous visits there. Neither the identity of the wrongdoer nor the nature of the offense is clear to us today, but it is very clear that Paul was deeply grieved. Perhaps he had been publicly humiliated or his authority had been challenged and the community had not supported him. In any case, Paul put off the next visit he had planned to make in Corinth and instead wrote a letter—one lost to us—urging the Corinthians to reprove the sinner and mend the situation (2 Corinthians 2:1,3-4). Now, assured that this had been accomplished and that he once again had the community's confidence (7:6-7,11), Paul asked them to be lenient and forgiving with the offender (2:6-11).

Often, when we have been injured or wronged, we would rather gloss over it because we find it uncomfortable to bring up with the person who has hurt us. Perhaps we even silently nurse a grudge, refusing to forgive or show mercy. There is much we can learn from how Paul dealt with an incident like this. While he charged the Corinthians to correct the wrongdoer, not ignoring the offense, he also implored them to "forgive and comfort him, or he may be overwhelmed by excessive sorrow" (2 Corinthians 2:7). He knew that if the community went out of its way to demonstrate their forgiveness, they would be reaffirming to the offender that they still did love him, just as Christ loved him (2:8).

Although Paul himself had been hurt, he remained sensitive to the one who had offended him. Paul recognized that forgiveness was a strong weapon against any attempt of Satan to divide the community and tempt the wrongdoer to despair of God's pardon. Aware of Satan's designs, he was forgiving and wanted the Corinthians to be as well, to keep evil from gaining any advantage over them (2 Corinthians 2:10-11). Reconciliation, Paul knew, was the way to prevent Satan from triumphing.

Paul forgave the person who wronged him in Corinth. Jesus forgave those who crucified him (Luke 23:34). God has forgiven our sins and shown us mercy. We, too, are called to "be kind to one another, tenderhearted, forgiving one another, as God in Christ forgave [us]" (Ephesians 4:32). As St. John Chrysostom wrote: "Nothing makes us so Godlike as our willingness to forgive."

"Jesus, I know you've asked me to forgive others as you have forgiven me. Help me, Lord, for without your help my heart is too small and unforgiving!"

2 Corinthians 2:12–3:3

[12] When I came to Tro'as to preach the gospel of Christ, a door was opened for me in the Lord; [13] but my mind could not rest because I did not find my brother Titus there. So I took leave of them and went on to Macedo'nia.

[14] But thanks be to God, who in Christ always leads us in triumph, and through us spreads the fragrance of the knowledge of him everywhere. [15] For we are the aroma of Christ to God among those who are being saved and among those who are perishing, [16] to one a fragrance from death to death, to the other a fragrance from life to life. Who is sufficient for these things? [17] For we are not, like so many, peddlers of God's word; but as men of sincerity, as commissioned by God, in the sight of God we speak in Christ.

[1] Are we beginning to commend ourselves again? Or do we need, as some do, letters of recommendation to you, or from you? [2] You yourselves are our letter of recommendation, written on your hearts, to

be known and read by all men; [3] and you show that you are a letter from Christ delivered by us, written not with ink but with the Spirit of the living God, not on tablets of stone but on tablets of human hearts.

After World War II ended, the streets of New York, London, and Paris filled with crowds of people who gathered to watch victory and homecoming parades of officers and their troops who had fought so valiantly. This is the kind of picture Paul intended to bring to mind when he wrote of his ministry to proclaim the gospel: "Thanks be to God, who in Christ always leads us in triumph, and through us spreads the fragrance of the knowledge of Christ" (2 Corinthians 2:14).

The Corinthians were familiar with "triumphs," or the triumphal processions of great generals when they paraded at the head of their armies on returning home from victorious campaigns. Thus, they could easily picture Paul's metaphor: Through the preaching of the gospel and its acceptance by those who hear it, God passes through the world in triumph. Since, in the ancient world, incense was commonly burned in these military parades, Paul further likened this spreading of the knowledge of God to the sweet smell of incense that filled the air as the conquering heroes progressed and was breathed in by the crowds lining their victory route.

Then Paul evoked yet another image with his metaphor, comparing himself and others who proclaim God's word to the aroma that arises from the burning of a sacrificial offering. Paul's life itself and his example of Christian living was a sacrifice offered to God—for the sake of those who would hear the word he preached and see the witness of his life: "For we are the aroma of Christ to God among those who are being saved and among those who are perishing" (2 Corinthians 2:15). To those who accept and embrace this message, it brings the sweet scent of life, and to those who reject it, the stench of death (2:16).

We, too, are called to being living witnesses of the gospel to our family, friends, neighbors, and coworkers. As St. Josemaría Escrivá once wrote in words that echo Paul's, "Every Christian should make Christ present among men. He ought to act in such a way that those who know him sense 'the aroma of Christ.' People should be able to recognize the Master in his disciples."

"Fill me with your Spirit, Lord. Give me courage to be your witness and speak your words to others with love and compassion. May many come to know you through what they see of your life in me."

2 Corinthians 3:4-14

[4] Such is the confidence that we have through Christ toward God. [5] Not that we are competent of ourselves to claim anything as coming from us; our competence is from God, [6] who has made us competent to be ministers of a new covenant, not in a written code but in the Spirit; for the written code kills, but the Spirit gives life.

[7] Now if the dispensation of death, carved in letters on stone, came with such splendor that the Israelites could not look at Moses' face because of its brightness, fading as this was, [8] will not the dispensation of the Spirit be attended with greater splendor? [9] For if there was splendor in the dispensation of condemnation, the dispensation of righteousness must far exceed it in splendor. [10] Indeed, in this case, what once had splendor has come to have no splendor at all, because of the splendor that surpasses it. [11] For if what faded away came with

splendor, what is permanent must have much more splendor.
[12] Since we have such a hope, we are very bold, [13] not like Moses, who put a veil over his face so that the Israelites might not see the end of the fading splendor. [14] But their minds were hardened; for to this day, when they read the old covenant, that same veil remains unlifted, because only through Christ is it taken away.

Some members of the Corinthian church resisted Paul's ministry and leadership. They considered him arrogant to assume such authority over them. The standards of leadership they held may have been false, but they measured Paul and the other apostles against them nonetheless. It was necessary, then, for Paul to challenge their thinking in a way that would focus attention on God and his work.

Paul drew a comparison between the glory of the old covenant given to Moses on Mt. Sinai and the greater glory of the new covenant inaugurated through the death and resurrection of Christ (2 Corinthians 3:7-8; Exodus 34:27-35). The old covenant was inaugurated with glory, for it was given by God to a people who received his name. But Paul said this glory faded because it reflected "the dispensation of condemnation," while the new covenant reflected "the dispensation of justification" (2 Corinthians 3:9).

This new covenant is "not in a written code but in the Spirit" (2 Corinthians 3:6). Sealed in Jesus' blood, the new covenant is eternal, offering us a whole new life. Through the new covenant, the Holy Spirit fills us with divine life and gives us new hearts of flesh, upon which is written the law of God. The Spirit empowers us to obey, love, and serve God and one another. The new covenant in Jesus is truly a covenant of life. This is the covenant Paul served; his competence in it came from God through "the Spirit [who] gives life" (3:6).

Through our baptism and faith in God, we too share in the covenant of life. This glorious privilege requires a response from us. We must daily seek God in prayer and the study of Scripture so that the Holy Spirit might immerse us in this new life. As we receive the Eucharist and love and serve one another, we also allow the Spirit to transform us. The response is up to us: God calls us and offers us a share in his life but we must choose daily. Let us commit our hearts to cooperate with the grace God is pouring out upon us.

"Lord Jesus, you are the author of the new covenant of life Paul was called to serve. I too want a share in this covenant. May your Spirit lead and teach me in the ways that will bring me ever closer to you."

2 Corinthians 3:15–4:6

[15] Yes, to this day whenever Moses is read a veil lies over their minds; [16] but when a man turns to the Lord the veil is removed. [17] Now the Lord is the Spirit, and where the Spirit of the Lord is, there is freedom. [18] And we all, with unveiled face, beholding the glory of the Lord, are being changed into his likeness from one degree of glory to another; for this comes from the Lord who is the Spirit.

[1] Therefore, having this ministry by the mercy of God, we do not lose heart. [2] We have renounced disgraceful, underhanded ways; we refuse to practice cunning or to tamper with God's word, but by the open statement of the truth we would commend ourselves to every man's conscience in the sight of God. [3] And even if our gospel is veiled, it is veiled only to those who are perishing. [4] In their case the

god of this world has blinded the minds of the unbelievers, to keep them from seeing the light of the gospel of the glory of Christ, who is the likeness of God. [5] For what we preach is not ourselves, but Jesus Christ as Lord, with ourselves as your servants for Jesus' sake. [6] For it is the God who said, "Let light shine out of darkness," who has shone in our hearts to give the light of the knowledge of the glory of God in the face of Christ.

In many ways, living the Christian life is like looking at light reflected in a mirror. As we pray, the light of Christ shines into our hearts and enables us to reflect that light to others. Yet, unlike reflections in a mirror, as we receive Jesus' light, we don't just reflect that light passively. We are actually "changed into his likeness" (2 Corinthians 3:18) as we take on Jesus' very nature and his attributes.

The Greek word Paul used to describe this change is *metamorphumetha*—or metamorphosis—which speaks of a transformation, not just a simple reflection. It's the same word, in fact, that the gospel writers used to describe the way Jesus looked at his Transfiguration (Matthew 17:2; Mark 9:2). The change that Paul was talking about, then, is not something small and incidental. It's a transformation that affects every aspect of our lives and moves us from an ordinary to an extraordinary way of living. Reflecting on his own experience of conversion and subsequent times of prayer (Acts 9:1-9; 2 Corinthians 4:6), Paul understood that no one can come into contact with the Lord and not be changed.

As he strove to respond to the Corinthians' suspicions and accusations, Paul distinguished between empty boasting and the humble yet secure confidence that comes from being changed into the likeness of Christ. He reminded them that everyone who looks to Jesus will experience this transformation. That's why Paul's confidence did not rest in himself (as the Corinthians wrongly assumed), but in the God who had brought about so radical a change in his life.

Just as he did for Paul, Jesus wants to transform us—and keep transforming us over time. He wants to dispel our fear and sin so that his light can shine more brightly, both in our hearts and out to the world. Paul understood that his calling to be an apostle was the result of God's mercy (2 Corinthians 4:1), and this knowledge kept him humble and dependent on the Lord. In the same way, God wants us to learn humility and trust in fulfilling our callings. He wants us to know that we can depend on him and never be disappointed. Let us continue to seek his revelation in prayer, entrusting him with our lives.

"Thank you, Father, that I can always come to you to receive your love. Do not let fear or guilt prevent me from seeking your Son's face in prayer. May I be changed and healed as I behold his glory."

2 Corinthians 4:7-18

[7] But we have this treasure in earthen vessels, to show that the transcendent power belongs to God and not to us. [8] We are afflicted in every way, but not crushed; perplexed, but not driven to despair; [9] persecuted, but not forsaken; struck down, but not destroyed; [10] always carrying in the body the death of Jesus, so that the life of Jesus may also be manifested in our bodies. [11] For while we live we are always being given up to death for Jesus' sake, so that the life of Jesus may be manifested in our mortal flesh. [12] So death is at work in us, but life in you.

[13] Since we have the same spirit of faith as he had who wrote, "I believed, and so I spoke," we too believe, and so we speak, [14] knowing that he who raised the Lord Jesus will raise us also with Jesus and bring us with you into his presence. [15] For it is all for your sake, so that as grace extends to more and more people it may increase thanksgiving, to the glory of God.
[16] So we do not lose heart. Though our outer nature is wasting away, our inner nature is being renewed every day. [17] For this slight momentary affliction is preparing for us an eternal weight of glory beyond all comparison, [18] because we look not to the things that are seen but to the things that are unseen; for the things that are seen are transient, but the things that are unseen are eternal.

What did Paul mean when he wrote about "carrying in the body the death of Jesus, so that the life of Jesus may also be manifested in our bodies" (2 Corinthians 4:10)? Is this just philosophical rhetoric? A stirring, but vague, discussion of suffering for the gospel?

Not at all. This is the heart of the gospel. When Jesus died and rose, he did it for us. In a sense, he took us with him to Calvary and now invites us to join him on the death-to-life trail that he blazed. When we were baptized, we were united with Jesus in his cross and resurrection, and now every day we are called to consider ourselves truly dead to sin and alive to God in Christ (Romans 6:3-11). It's as we daily unite ourselves with Jesus' death—saying no to sin and yes to his Holy Spirit—that we receive more and more of the divine life that God longs to give us.

We need only reflect on our own efforts to change our hearts to know that we need God's "transcendent power" if we want to become like Jesus (2 Corinthians 4:7). We are all too familiar with the drives toward anger, selfishness, lust, and resentment that lurk in our hearts. How we long to be free of them! How peaceful our lives would be without such burdens! And this is exactly where Paul's "death-to-life" principle applies.

To "carry the death of Jesus" means to keep our union with him on the cross in the forefront of our minds. It means to recall throughout the day that Jesus really has set us free and that we don't have to live as orphans anymore. It means to see the cross as the precious treasure that we carry in the earthen vessels of our hearts—the all-powerful life of Jesus at work in us daily, changing us and filling us with his character.

Take the death of Jesus with you today. Thank him for his cross and acknowledge it as the power to change your heart. When you experience temptation moving in you, proclaim in faith that you are crucified with Jesus and that Christ lives in you (Galatians 2:20). Trust that just as his death is at work in you, so too is his life—flowing from within your heart and touching others with the love of God himself.

"Jesus, thank you for dying for me so that I could be redeemed and filled with your life. Your death and resurrection are the power through which I can be set free from sin and display your life—your love, joy, and goodness—to others. By your Spirit, make these truths a reality in my life today."

2 Corinthians 5:1-10

[1] For we know that if the earthly tent we live in is destroyed, we have a building from God, a house not made with hands, eternal in the heavens. [2] Here indeed we groan, and long to put on our heavenly dwelling, [3] so that by putting it on we may not be found naked. [4] For

while we are still in this tent, we sigh with anxiety; not that we would be unclothed, but that we would be further clothed, so that what is mortal may be swallowed up by life. [5] He who has prepared us for this very thing is God, who has given us the Spirit as a guarantee.

[6] So we are always of good courage; we know that while we are at home in the body we are away from the Lord, [7] for we walk by faith, not by sight. [8] We are of good courage, and we would rather be away from the body and at home with the Lord. [9] So whether we are at home or away, we make it our aim to please him. [10] For we must all appear before the judgment seat of Christ, so that each one may receive good or evil, according to what he has done in the body.

How easy it can be to get caught up in our everyday activities—to the point that we lose sight of our future destiny! Yet as Christians, we know we are only sojourners passing through this world for a short time. We are nothing more than "strangers and exiles on the earth," pilgrims on the way to our heavenly "homeland" (Hebrews 11:13-14).

As he continued to explain and defend his ministry to the people of Corinth, Paul likened our earthly existence to living in a temporary shelter, like a tent. Some of Paul's actions, and some of the ways he related to the Corinthian Christians, seemed odd to them, he said, because they were expecting him to act as someone whose eyes are fixed only on this world. That's why Paul emphasized that his destination—as well as theirs—was heaven, an eternal dwelling place with God (2 Corinthians 5:1). One day, as Paul assured the Corinthians, "we shall all be changed, in a moment, in the twinkling of an eye, at the last trumpet. . . . For this perishable nature must put on the imperishable, and this mortal nature must put on immortality" (1 Corinthians 15:51-53).

Paul is not the only one to have recognized our present condition as transitory. Throughout the history of the church, a roster of saints and spiritual writers have compared our earthly life to a journey, urging us to keep our eyes fixed on heaven. St. Alphonsus Liguori wrote: "This in not our fatherland; we are here, as it were, passing through, like pilgrims. . . . Our fatherland is heaven, which we have to merit by God's grace and our own good actions. Our home is not the one we live in at present, which serves only as a temporary dwelling; our home is eternity."

St. John Vianney, the Curé of Ars, expressed the same point with remarkable simplicity: "Our home is—heaven. On earth we are like travelers staying in a hotel. When one is away, one is always thinking of going home." Finally, St. Thérèse of Lisieux wrote: "The country in which I live is not my native country. That lies elsewhere, and it must always be the center of my longings."

God wants our hope in heaven to give us courage, confidence, and a sense of security in the midst of our daily difficulties (2 Corinthians 5:6-8). And, so we don't forget what lies ahead, the Holy Spirit has been given to us as a "guarantee"—a down payment—of the life that we shall someday have in its fullness (5:5).

"Lord, for your faithful people life is changed, not ended. When the body of our earthly dwelling lies in death, we gain an everlasting dwelling place in heaven" (*Roman Missal*, *Mass for the Dead*, Preface).

2 Corinthians 5:11-19

[11] Therefore, knowing the fear of the Lord, we persuade men; but what we are is known to God, and I hope it is known also to your conscience. [12] We are not commending ourselves to you again but giving you cause to be proud of us, so that you may be able to answer those who pride themselves on a man's position and not on his heart. [13] For if we are beside ourselves, it is for God; if we are in our right mind, it is for you. [14] For the love of Christ controls us, because we are convinced that one has died for all; therefore all have died. [15] And he died for all, that those who live might live no longer for themselves but for him who for their sake died and was raised.

[16] From now on, therefore, we regard no one from a human point of view; even though we once regarded Christ from a human point of view, we regard him thus no longer. [17] Therefore, if any one is in Christ, he is a new creation; the old has passed away, behold, the new has come. [18] All this is from God, who through Christ reconciled us to himself and gave us the ministry of reconciliation; [19] that is, in Christ God was reconciling the world to himself, not counting their trespasses against them, and entrusting to us the message of reconciliation.

Responding to accusations against his work as an apostle, Paul defended himself by presenting Jesus' all-consuming love as the basis for his actions and decisions (2 Corinthians 5:14). This love of Christ, Paul wrote, "controls" those who are touched by it. It is not a binding power that manipulates people like puppets.

Rather, it is a compelling force that transforms the heart of the believer and fills him or her with a desire to please the Lord.

What is so compelling about Jesus' love? "One died for all; therefore all have died" (2 Corinthians 5:14). Jesus' death canceled the unpaid—and unpayable—debt that we owed our Creator. Jesus Christ, the innocent and perfect Son of God, took upon himself the punishment that our sins deserved (5:19). All is forgiven. We are freed from guilt and now live under God's unfathomable mercy.

What incredible love! No more guilt, no more separation from God our Father. Now we can experience his love personally, intimately. The power that Satan held over our lives because of sin have been revoked. Now we can live as a new creation, no longer slaves to sin and death, but beloved sons and daughters of God.

God's love compelled Paul to devote his life to those who had never heard the good news of Jesus' death and resurrection. No longer looking at people "from a human point of view" (2 Corinthians 5:16), Paul looked at them with the eyes of God. Distinctions between rich and poor, Gentile and Jew, slave and free, no longer applied (Galatians 3:28). The only question was whether a person had become a "new creation" in Christ. No wonder Paul willingly took up the call to be an ambassador of Christ, despite its hardships! We too have received this calling, whether it is to proclaim this wonderful news to the nations or to our close friends. Like Paul, let us embrace the call with grateful, eager hearts.

"Jesus, by your death and resurrection, you have made me a new creation. May the joy of this new creation burn in my heart and move me to embrace all your promises. Set my heart on fire with your love and compel me to spread the glorious news that everyone can be made new in Christ."

2 Corinthians 5:20–6:2

[20] So we are ambassadors for Christ, God making his appeal through us. We beseech you on behalf of Christ, be reconciled to God. [21] For our sake he made him to be sin who knew no sin, so that in him we might become the righteousness of God.

[1] Working together with him, then, we entreat you not to accept the grace of God in vain. [2] For he says,

"At the acceptable time I have listened to you,
and helped you on the day of salvation."

Behold, now is the acceptable time; behold, now is the day of salvation.

We entreat you not to accept the grace of God in vain.
(2 Corinthians 6:1)

This blessed invitation has echoed across the centuries, and it will continue to resound until the Second Coming. So how do we accept this "grace of God," and what is it that this grace is meant to accomplish in us?

God respects the freedom he has given us as his creatures. He invites, asks, even entreats us to draw near to him. He longs to see us rend our hearts, and not our garments, in humble repentance (Joel 2:13). He rejoices when we demonstrate an attitude like the psalmist's, acknowledging our sin and God's justice, and bringing the acceptable sacrifice of a broken and contrite heart (Psalm 51:16-17).

God does not hold out specific tasks for us to perform, without which we will have no hope of experiencing his grace. As we examine our lives, each of us will come to see what is required of us. For the rich young man, the challenge was to overcome his strong attachment to his wealth (Mark 10:17-22). For the prodigal son, the challenge was to recognize how much his father loved him (Luke 15:11-32). And for the woman caught in adultery, the challenge was to put aside her sin so that the mercy of God could change her life (John 8:1-11).

No matter what we need to do in order to receive God's grace, we must remember that ultimately it is God himself who makes us capable of saying "yes" to him. After all, he is the one who made Jesus Christ, his sinless and perfect Son, "to be sin" for us, so that his redeeming love could penetrate our hearts and transform us into "the righteousness of God" (2 Corinthians 5:21). It's as we allow his light to shine in our darkness that we can be raised above the limitations and impotence of a humanity darkened by sin. This was the point the Corinthians were missing as they pursued their own "wisdom teaching" and upheld their own criteria by which they would judge Paul.

This generosity of God in showing us how to cooperate with his transforming power is the grace Paul prays we will never receive in vain. Our human cooperation may seem insignificant compared to the power of God to change us, but it is still vitally necessary. At its heart it remains primarily the all-encompassing power of God at work in our limited, human lives. May this invitation never fall on deaf ears or hardened hearts!

"Heavenly Father, with the freedom you have given me, I say 'yes' to your invitation! May each day now be a new 'day of salvation,' bringing me a deeper knowledge and experience of your life."

2 Corinthians 6:3-13

[3] We put no obstacle in any one's way, so that no fault may be found with our ministry, [4] but as servants of God we commend ourselves in every way: through great endurance, in afflictions, hardships, calamities, [5] beatings, imprisonments, tumults, labors, watching, hunger; [6] by purity, knowledge, forbearance, kindness, the Holy Spirit, genuine love, [7] truthful speech, and the power of God; with the weapons of righteousness for the right hand and for the left; [8] in honor and dishonor, in ill repute and good repute. We are treated as impostors, and yet are true; [9] as unknown, and yet well known; as dying, and behold we live; as punished, and yet not killed; [10] as sorrowful, yet always rejoicing; as poor, yet making many rich; as having nothing, and yet possessing everything.
[11] Our mouth is open to you, Corinthians; our heart is wide. [12] You are not restricted by us, but you are restricted in your own affections. [13] In return — I speak as to children — widen your hearts also.

There are parts of Paul's letters that make him sound almost superhuman as he writes about all that he has endured as an apostle. A closer reading, however, shows that it was only by staying close to the Holy Spirit and relying on the power of God that Paul was able to persevere and accomplish all he did (2 Corinthians 6:6-7). In his Letter to the Philippians, for example, he wrote: "I have learned the secret of facing plenty and hunger, abundance and want. I can do all things in him who strengthens me" (Philippians 4:12-13). Paul's success did not come primarily from his own resources, but from a humble reliance on Christ in him, his hope of glory (Colossians 1:27)

Like all of us, Paul faced challenging situations that demanded difficult decisions. He could either rely on his own strength and knowledge or bring his concerns to the Lord for discernment and guidance. Paul's ability to act so confidently, then, was the result of the many opportunities he had to practice the balance between going to God for wisdom and strength, and trusting in God's grace enough to forge ahead.

After Paul's dramatic conversion, the Christians in Jerusalem were afraid of him because they knew him only as a persecutor (Acts 9:26). Paul, however, didn't allow their perception of him to keep him from preaching the gospel. When his work as an apostle brought hardship and suffering across his path, he carried on because he wanted to share the love of Christ with as many people as he could. Even when he had to defend himself against false charges, Paul knew that God would not abandon him. And so, he did not back down.

A brief review of Paul's life story demonstrates that he was not attracted to the missionary life because it was glamorous or because it helped him build an impressive résumé among his fellow Pharisees. If that were the case, he would not have remained faithful to the Corinthians when they accused him of hypocrisy and selfish motivations. Like every missionary who would follow in his footsteps, the attraction was love: Christ's love in him flowing out to others just as freely as he had received it.

"Heavenly Father, help me lay my burdens at your feet, that you might guide me, empower me, and make me into a humble servant. By your Spirit, help me to trust that there is nothing I cannot accomplish in you, my strength."

2 Corinthians 6:14-18

[14] Do not be mismated with unbelievers. For what partnership have righteousness and iniquity? Or what fellowship has light with darkness? [15] What accord has Christ with Be'lial? Or what has a believer in common with an unbeliever? [16] What agreement has the temple of God with idols? For we are the temple of the living God; as God said,

"I will live in them and move among them,
and I will be their God,
and they shall be my people.
[17] Therefore come out from them,
and be separate from them, says the Lord,
and touch nothing unclean;
then I will welcome you,
[18] and I will be a father to you, and you shall be my sons
and daughters,
says the Lord Almighty."

You've never seen a farmer plowing his field with a horse and an ox yoked side by side to the plow, have you? Of course not! What folly that would be, since two such different, mismatched animals would not be able to pull the plow well together and make a deep, straight furrow. Well, this is just the picture Paul purposefully drew for the Corinthians—recalling the Old Testament injunction, "You shall not plow with an ox and an ass together" (Deuteronomy 22:10)—to show them the folly of the behavior they seemed close to falling back into. When they had accepted the gospel, the believers in Corinth had made a decisive change in their way of living. But now Paul was concerned that they not revert to former sinful or pagan practices.

The gospel makes a real difference: When a Christian breaks with unbelief and past sin, he takes on the mind of Christ. In a sense, the believer is a different "species" from the unbeliever, and can no longer live like those without faith (2 Corinthians 6:14,17). Paul used several other contrasting images in addition to that of a mismatched team to illustrate his point: Light has nothing to do with darkness, just as righteousness is opposed to lawlessness (6:14). The worship of idols has nothing in common with the worship of the one true God (6:16).

Through these graphic examples—all powerful statements of God's holiness and the exclusiveness of his claims on the believer—Paul made it clear that following Christ and the gospel is incompatible with sin. The Corinthians had to decide: Either embrace God's way of holiness or the ways of Belial—a name for Satan commonly used in Jewish literature—since a believer can't be on both sides (2 Corinthians 6:15).

Through his exhortation, Paul was also warning the Corinthians of the dangers of failing to recognize the true ministers of God and of misinterpreting their ministry. In other words, he was telling them that they were on dangerous ground spiritually when they used the wrong criteria to judge true apostleship. By judging Paul and his companions falsely or bringing unfounded accusations against them, they would produce division and animosity in the community. Such behavior—whether against him or any other member of the church—grieved Paul, not only because it hurt him personally but because of the ill effects it would have on the whole church in Corinth.

When we fall into similar judgmental attitudes toward church leaders or believe unsubstantiated accusations against fellow believers, we run the same risks the Corinthians did. We obscure our experience of

God's presence among us, and so weaken our ability to witness to the world as a people of the resurrection. Let us, then, ask God's forgiveness for any ways we have acted wrongly toward our brothers and sisters in Christ or judged them falsely.

Repentance and Generosity

2 CORINTHIANS 7–9

2 Corinthians 7:1-10

[1] Since we have these promises, beloved, let us cleanse ourselves from every defilement of body and spirit, and make holiness perfect in the fear of God.

[2] Open your hearts to us; we have wronged no one, we have corrupted no one, we have taken advantage of no one. [3] I do not say this to condemn you, for I said before that you are in our hearts, to die together and to live together. [4] I have great confidence in you; I have great pride in you; I am filled with comfort. With all our affliction, I am overjoyed.

[5] For even when we came into Macedo'nia, our bodies had no rest but we were afflicted at every turn — fighting without and fear within. [6] But God, who comforts the downcast, comforted us by the coming of Titus, [7] and not only by his coming but also by the comfort with which he was comforted in you, as he told us of your longing, your mourning, your zeal for me, so that I rejoiced still more. [8] For even if I made you sorry with my letter, I do not regret it (though I did regret it), for I see that that letter grieved you, though only for a while. [9] As it is, I rejoice, not because you were grieved, but because you were grieved into repenting; for you felt a godly grief, so that you suffered no loss through us. [10] For godly grief produces a repentance that leads to salvation and brings no regret, but worldly grief produces death.

One of the greatest modern examples of reconciliation occurred when Pope John Paul II met with Mehmet Ali Agca, his would-be assassin, and spoke to him in prison. The image was captured on film and made its way into newspapers and onto television sets throughout the world. Not only did the pope meet with Agca, he prayed with him and assured the man he had forgiven him. Can you imagine trying to make peace with someone who had tried to kill you? What kind of spiritual conviction that would take!

Repentance, forgiveness, and reconciliation are not always easy, even when the offenses are far smaller than an assassination attempt! Most of us find it very difficult to connect again with people who have slandered us or treated us cruelly in some way. This is exactly what happened to St. Paul. Some members of the church in Corinth had begun spreading vicious rumors about his integrity as an apostle, and many others began to believe them. Yet, as passionately as Paul defended himself, he was just as passionate in seeking unity and reconciliation again with these people.

As Christians, we are called to try our best to be at peace with everyone in our lives. Even when the hurt is grievous, God's call remains: Seek peace. Aim for reconciliation. Forgive just as fully as you have been forgiven. Take as your example Jesus, who forgave even those who had just nailed him to the cross.

This teaching can seem awfully hard, and on the basis of human effort alone, it can even be impossible. But that's not the way God intended us to live. He never wants to see us attempting any aspect of the Christian life—especially the most challenging ones like forgiveness—by our own strength. He knows that such efforts will only end in disappointment, or even disaster. That's why he gave us the Holy Spirit.

Have you been hurt by someone? Are you finding it hard to forgive past wrongs or sins committed against you? Do you find yourself occasionally caught in a pool of anger, depression, or fear because of such things? Turn to the Holy Spirit and ask him to shine the love and mercy of God into your heart. Beg him for a deeper revelation of the mercy that was shown to you so that you can be just as merciful yourself. Go to the Scriptures and read such stories as the prodigal son (Luke 15:11-32), the woman caught in adultery (John 8:1-11), and the unmerciful steward (Matthew 18:23-34). Then, trusting in the Spirit's strength, take the next step toward reconciliation. Don't try to do it all at once. Just let the Spirit help you move closer to your goal. And the closer you get, the more peace and relief you'll experience.

"Jesus, by your Holy Spirit, teach me how to forgive. May I become an instrument of your peace in the world."

2 Corinthians 7:11-16

[11] For see what earnestness this godly grief has produced in you, what eagerness to clear yourselves, what indignation, what alarm, what longing, what zeal, what punishment! At every point you have proved yourselves guiltless in the matter. [12] So although I wrote to you, it was not on account of the one who did the wrong, nor on account of the one who suffered the wrong, but in order that your zeal for us might be revealed to you in the sight of God. [13] Therefore we are comforted.

And besides our own comfort we rejoiced still more at the joy of Titus, because his mind has been set at rest by you all. [14] For if I have expressed to him some pride in you, I was not put to shame; but just as everything we said to you was true, so our boasting before Titus has proved true. [15] And his heart goes out all the more to you, as he remembers the obedience of you all, and the fear and trembling with which you received him. [16] I rejoice, because I have perfect confidence in you.

Second Corinthians contains some of Paul's most passionate words of self-defense, words that convey how deeply hurt he felt by people he had loved so much. Other parts of this letter contain some of his sharpest rebukes, aimed at believers who were not only questioning his integrity but ignoring the call of the gospel as well. So why would he tell these recalcitrant men and women he has "complete confidence" in them?

Paul's excitement and joy are the result of having learned that the people of Corinth had indeed repented and were eager to be reconciled to him once more. His anxious waiting was over. Titus had returned from Corinth with the news that the letter Paul had sent earlier had the right effect and caused the people there to come back to him. You can practically hear the relief and exuberance in his voice—even as you suspect that things may not really have been as perfect as Paul would have liked to believe. It's possible that Paul had similar suspicions, but for the moment, he seemed to be too excited to care.

There is a lesson here. We can be quick to portray saints and biblical characters in stark black or white. Pontius Pilate, for example, is hopelessly weak. Or Moses was nothing short of a superhero all the time. But passages like this one show us that all these characters were flesh-and-blood humans just like us who felt pain and joy just as deeply as we do—and sometimes over the same small things that affect us.

How do you think about the heroes and heroines of faith? Do you see them as just as weak and vulnerable to sin as you are? Do you see them as just as subject to emotional swings as you can be? The saints weren't perfect. The only thing that set them apart was their determination to cling to Jesus and let him continue to work in their lives. Any one of us can do that as well. Any one of us can become just as holy as the greatest saint. All it takes is a little persistence and the willingness to repent when we fail. Let's not sell ourselves short. Even more to the point, let's not sell Jesus short by thinking he's not powerful enough to transform us. God isn't looking for the smartest, the strongest, or the bravest. He's only looking for regular people who will pray and take a few steps closer to him every day. He's looking for you!

2 Corinthians 8:1-15

[1] We want you to know, brethren, about the grace of God which has been shown in the churches of Macedo'nia, [2] for in a severe test of affliction, their abundance of joy and their extreme poverty have overflowed in a wealth of liberality on their part. [3] For they gave according to their means, as I can testify, and beyond their means, of their own free will, [4] begging us earnestly for the favor of taking part in the relief of the saints — [5] and this, not as we expected, but first they gave themselves to the Lord and to us by the will of God. [6] Accordingly we have urged Titus that as he had already made a beginning, he should also complete among you this gracious work. [7] Now as you excel in everything — in faith, in utterance, in knowledge, in all earnestness, and in your love for us — see that you excel in this gracious work also. [8] I say this not as a command, but to prove by the earnestness of others that your love also is genuine. [9] For you know the grace of our Lord Jesus Christ, that though he was rich, yet for your sake he became poor, so that by his poverty you might become rich. [10] And in this matter I give my advice: it is best for you now to complete what a year ago you began not only to do but to desire,[11] so that your readiness in

desiring it may be matched by your completing it out of what you have. [12] For if the readiness is there, it is acceptable according to what a man has, not according to what he has not. [13] I do not mean that others should be eased and you burdened, [14] but that as a matter of equality your abundance at the present time should supply their want, so that their abundance may supply your want, that there may be equality. [15] As it is written, "He who gathered much had nothing over, and he who gathered little had no lack."

Troubles stemming from suspicion and persecution continually harassed the Christian community in Jerusalem. Paul initiated the taking up of a collection among the gentile Christians as a means not only to bring material relief to the Jerusalem Christians but to encourage unity between Gentile and Jewish believers.

The Greeks in Macedonia had given far beyond their means to Paul's appeal for funds, and Paul mentioned this to the more wealthy Corinthians, hoping to spur them to a similar generosity. He said that their giving should be a response to "the generous act of our Lord Jesus Christ, that though he was rich . . . he became poor, so that by his poverty you might become rich" (2 Corinthians 8:9).

In the Old Testament, almsgiving was seen as a human effort to imitate the goodness and kindness of God. Laws made provision for all classes of people in need—orphans, widows, the homeless and oppressed, aliens, the hungry and thirsty. Prophets and psalmists alike repeatedly reminded that the cry of the poor demanded a generous response (Isaiah 58:7; Zechariah 7:10; Psalm 146:5-9).

Jesus identified with the poor and told people wishing to be perfect to sell what they owned and give to the poor, then come and follow him (Matthew 19:21). Jesus is calling us to respond generously to our less fortunate brothers and sisters as we encounter them. Whatever our circumstances, most of us are probably better provided for than millions of others in the world. We must remember that everything we have is a gift from God, given not just for own security, but that we might share liberally with others according to our abilities.

Our faith in Jesus Christ is the most precious gift we have to share; bringing others to know Jesus and his love must be our first priority. As we share our faith, the Holy Spirit will turn our hearts toward others and help us to see their material needs as well. The Spirit of God will touch us and begin to dissipate our self-concern. We will begin to see Christ calling us to be one in him. And as a result, we will want to give of ourselves and of our wealth so that we can share deeply in this oneness.

2 Corinthians 8:16-24

[16] But thanks be to God who puts the same earnest care for you into the heart of Titus. [17] For he not only accepted our appeal, but being himself very earnest he is going to you of his own accord. [18] With him we are sending the brother who is famous among all the churches for his preaching of the gospel; [19] and not only that, but he has been appointed by the churches to travel with us in this gracious work which we are carrying on, for the glory of the Lord and to show our good will. [20] We intend that no one should blame us about this liberal gift which we are administering, [21] for we aim at what is

honorable not only in the Lord's sight but also in the sight of men. [22] And with them we are sending our brother whom we have often tested and found earnest in many matters, but who is now more earnest than ever because of his great confidence in you. [23] As for Titus, he is my partner and fellow worker in your service; and as for our brethren, they are messengers of the churches, the glory of Christ. [24] So give proof, before the churches, of your love and of our boasting about you to these men.

"A few good men"—a trio of them, actually—undertook the task of delivering the Corinthians' gift to its beneficiaries, the needy church in Jerusalem. Titus, a non-Jewish Christian (Galatians 2:3), may have been one of the many young men Paul won to Christ—Paul called him his "true child" in the faith (Titus 1:4). We don't know the name of the second man, whom the church appointed for this errand (2 Corinthians 8:19), but Paul described him in glowing terms as "the brother who is famous among all the churches for his preaching of the gospel" (8:18). The third companion was, in Paul's opinion, well-tested and earnest, and one who held the Corinthians in high regard (8:22).

Paul was happy that the responsibility of delivering the funds had been delegated to such sound and reputable men since he was aware that his relationship with the Corinthians had been strained and was still delicate. The three men's presence on the trip would ensure that Paul's involvement with the collection was above reproach or suspicion and would safeguard him against any criticisms from the Corinthians or accusations of embezzlement (2 Corinthians 8:20).

Titus shared Paul's love and concern for the Corinthians (2 Corinthians 7:6,13,14; 8:16). A gifted and capable leader, he had helped Paul bring the Corinthian church through a difficult time of scandal and dissension (7:15). Counting on the Corinthians' love and generosity, Titus volunteered to take up the collection (8:17). If you've ever been involved in fund-raising or making appeals for money on behalf of the needy, you know such work can be daunting. All the more then can we appreciate Titus' character. Concerned for his needy brothers and sisters in Jerusalem, he had a great love for them and desire to help them. It's also worth noting that Paul appointed Titus the first bishop of the church in Crete, where he carried out his responsibilities wisely and competently (Titus 1–3).

Titus willingly took on the job of soliciting donations from the Corinthians—and carried the job out in love. A good role model, his example shows us how to offer our gifts and abilities to the Lord generously so that we can be of service to those in need. Every good work we do—no matter how small or great, hidden or visible—is valuable to the Lord and cherished by him. Our generosity of heart is what pleases God most, and this is what releases his blessing most powerfully.

"Father, widen my heart so that I will desire to serve others with my talents, energy, and time. You have been so generous in loving and blessing me. Help me to be generous as well."

2 Corinthians 9:1-9

[1] Now it is superfluous for me to write to you about the offering for the saints, [2] for I know your readiness, of which I boast about you to the people of Macedo'nia, saying that Acha'ia has been ready since last year; and your zeal has stirred up most of them. [3] But I am sending the brethren so that our boasting about you may not prove vain in

this case, so that you may be ready, as I said you would be;
[4] lest if some Macedo'nians come with me and find that you are not ready, we be humiliated — to say nothing of you — for being so confident. [5] So I thought it necessary to urge the brethren to go on to you before me, and arrange in advance for this gift you have promised, so that it may be ready not as an exaction but as a willing gift.

[6] The point is this: he who sows sparingly will also reap sparingly, and he who sows bountifully will also reap bountifully. [7] Each one must do as he has made up his mind, not reluctantly or under compulsion, for God loves a cheerful giver. [8] And God is able to provide you with every blessing in abundance, so that you may always have enough of everything and may provide in abundance for every good work.
[9] As it is written,

> "He scatters abroad, he gives to the poor;
> his righteousness endures for ever."

"The Christian should never worry about tomorrow or give sparingly because of a possible future need." George Mueller (1805-1898), a great evangelist and servant of God in Britain, wrote these words in 1852, a year in which he was praying for funds to provide a home for orphaned children. In 1857, he opened that home, the first of many he would build, without ever soliciting money from anyone.

Mueller sowed abundantly by persevering in prayer, asking the Lord to provide for the needy. He reaped abundantly, not just in terms of money he received or facilities he established, but in the harvest from the lives of children who were rescued from poverty and suffering. They were loved and instructed and, in turn, went on to produce works for the Lord.

St. Paul exhorted the Corinthians to sow abundantly by generously giving to the needy church in Jerusalem. In the same way that a farmer makes an investment by sowing a certain amount of seed, anyone who gives time, money, service, or possessions to care for the needy is certain to receive an even greater reward in return (2 Corinthians 9:6-8,11).

St. John Chrysostom (c. 347-407) responded to such great promises and clear commands by crying out:

> Let us not nicely calculate, but sow with a profuse hand. Don't you see how much others give to players and harlots? Give at any rate the half to Christ, of what they give to dancers.

Never one to mince words, Chrysostom continued:

> As long as you spend it [your money] on your belly and on drunkenness and dissipation, you never think of poverty; but when need is to relieve poverty, you become poorer than anybody. And when feeding parasites and flatterers, you're as joyous as though you had fountains to spend from; but if you chance to see a poor man, then the fear of poverty besets you. (*Homilies on Second Corinthians*, 19:3)

In Jesus' name, let us set aside a portion of our income to give to the needy. Consider as well how we might give some of our most precious commodity—our time—and apply it to prayer and service for the needs of others.

"Lord Jesus, help me to be a generous giver. Give me the confidence to trust that you will care for me even as I give from what I have to those in need."

2 Corinthians 9:10-15

[10] He who supplies seed to the sower and bread for food will supply and multiply your resources and increase the harvest of your righteousness. [11] You will be enriched in every way for great generosity, which through us will produce thanksgiving to God; [12] for the rendering of this service not only supplies the wants of the saints but also overflows in many thanksgivings to God. [13] Under the test of this service, you will glorify God by your obedience in acknowledging the gospel of Christ, and by the generosity of your contribution for them and for all others; [14] while they long for you and pray for you, because of the surpassing grace of God in you. [15] Thanks be to God for his inexpressible gift!

When Paul wrote to the Corinthians of the principles and blessings of giving generously, he reminded them of the law God had given to the Israelites centuries earlier and the good consequences of following it: "You shall give to [your poor brother] freely, and your heart shall not be grudging when you give to him; because for this the LORD your God will bless you in all your work and in all that you undertake" (Deuteronomy 15:10).

When a gift is given unsparingly and with a glad heart, there are multiple benefactors: The recipients' needs are met, and the giver knows the joy of having been provided for by God as well as sharing with others the gifts he has received. In other words, generosity itself is its own reward, both for the one who receives and for the one who gives (2 Corinthians 9:10-11). "Almsgiving is called a 'blessing,'" St. Thomas Aquinas noted, "because it is the cause of eternal blessing.

For by the action of giving, the person is blessed by God and by men." Moreover, generous giving evokes thanksgiving to God from both the giver and the receiver (9:11-12). And, finally, God is glorified by such acts of generosity (9:13).

Christian generosity is not a matter only of doing the right thing, nor is it simply a footnote to the gospel. The generosity to which Paul was exhorting the Corinthians is at the heart of Christianity. Jesus is the Father's generous gift to us. Jesus made the most generous gift possible—the gift of his life—by offering himself on the cross for our sake. As one medieval commentator noted, "Jesus Christ is the example of generosity. Our Lord, because he is God, was in need of nothing; but by becoming man he voluntarily despoiled himself of the splendor of his divinity and lived on earth as a poor man—from his birth in poverty in Bethlehem to his death on the cross."

Jesus asks us to give generously—of ourselves and of what God has given to us. He has freed us not for self-indulgence but for loving and caring for other people. The Holy Spirit wants to empower you in little daily acts of generosity—"going the extra mile" (Matthew 5:41) and "giving to those in need" (Ephesians 4:28). Lending a helping hand to a coworker, supporting the work of a missionary in West Africa, bringing a meal to a sick neighbor, taking time during a busy day to call a lonely relative—these are all ways to "do good, to be rich in good deeds, liberal and generous." And they're the way to lay up "a good foundation for the future, so that [we] may take hold of the life which is life indeed" (1 Timothy 6:18-19).

"Father, every good gift comes from your hands. Thank you for allowing me to share in your blessings. Teach me to be generous in sharing those blessings with others."

Paul's Self-Defense

2 Corinthians 10–13

2 Corinthians 10:1-6

[1] I, Paul, myself entreat you, by the meekness and gentleness of Christ — I who am humble when face to face with you, but bold to you when I am away! — [2] I beg of you that when I am present I may not have to show boldness with such confidence as I count on showing against some who suspect us of acting in worldly fashion. [3] For though we live in the world we are not carrying on a worldly war, [4] for the weapons of our warfare are not worldly but have divine power to destroy strongholds. [5] We destroy arguments and every proud obstacle to the knowledge of God, and take every thought captive to obey Christ, [6] being ready to punish every disobedience, when your obedience is complete.

When asked about how he wanted to act toward those whom other church leaders had been quick to condemn, Blessed John XXIII was said to have replied, "Let us correct a little, overlook much, and observe all." Pope John was willing to give people the benefit of the doubt while he kept his eyes open to see if the fruit of the Spirit—love, peace, and kindness—were evident in their lives. Aware of his own shortcomings, he was careful not to judge other people against a more difficult standard than he had been judged.

Despite his sometimes passionate reactions to unsettling news, St. Paul had a similar view to John XXIII's. When Paul heard that some members of the Corinthian church had accused him of not being a true apostle of Jesus, he could have lashed out in unforgiving anger and resentment. Yet he didn't. Instead, he expressed his passion and sense of hurt in a way that led the people to repentance and change. Not waging war "according to human standards" of anger, resentment, and revenge, Paul chose instead to bring his thoughts under the authority of Christ—and to help the Corinthians do the same thing (2 Corinthians 10:3,5). And as a result, his words—which were direct but humble—actually brought healing and reconciliation.

Correction has a place in our lives, too. Parenting magazines will sometimes speak of "tough love," but perhaps a better phrase might be "firm love." Firm love disciplines a child when necessary, but is always careful to show the child love and respect. Isn't this the way all of us should treat each other?

Jesus also told us that if we need to correct someone, we should first seek to do it in private (Matthew 18:15). That way, the person being corrected will not feel belittled or humiliated. Instead, his or her dignity will be upheld, and he or she will have a far greater chance of accepting the correction in the spirit of love in which it was offered.

None of us is perfect, and so none of us is beyond correction. Let us pray that we can be open and humble whenever it is offered to us, whether by God or by someone close to us. In addition, let us also seek to correct ourselves through a regular examination of conscience and the grace of the Sacrament of Reconciliation.

May mercy and gentleness become the constant goal of our lives. May the words of the Beatitudes echo in our hearts and in our actions: "Blessed are the merciful, for they shall obtain mercy."

2 Corinthians 10:7-18

[7] Look at what is before your eyes. If any one is confident that he is Christ's, let him remind himself that as he is Christ's, so are we. [8] For even if I boast a little too much of our authority, which the Lord gave for building you up and not for destroying you, I shall not be put to shame. [9] I would not seem to be frightening you with letters. [10] For they say, "His letters are weighty and strong, but his bodily presence is weak, and his speech of no account." [11] Let such people understand that what we say by letter when absent, we do when present. [12] Not that we venture to class or compare ourselves with some of those who commend themselves. But when they measure themselves by one another, and compare themselves with one another, they are without understanding.

[13] But we will not boast beyond limit, but will keep to the limits God has apportioned us, to reach even to you. [14] For we are not overextending ourselves, as though we did not reach you; we were the first to come all the way to you with the gospel of Christ. [15] We do not boast beyond limit, in other men's labors; but our hope is that as your faith increases, our field among you may be greatly enlarged, [16] so that we may preach the gospel in lands beyond you, without boasting of work already done in another's field. [17] "Let him who boasts, boast of the Lord." [18] For it is not the man who commends himself that is accepted, but the man whom the Lord commends.

A high school teacher walked into her classroom one day and started the lesson with a provocative question: "Who of you in this room are humble?" One student immediately raised his hand, and with a smirk on his face, said, "I'm humble, and I'm very proud of it!"

Situations in the church in Corinth had pushed Paul to the point that he felt he had to "boast" of his qualifications as an apostle. He spoke of how God had worked in him and through him in powerful ways, and of how he had earned the title "apostle" fairly. The difference between Paul's boasting and the wisecracking student in the previous paragraph is that Paul was always quick to give God all the credit for his abilities. As far as Paul was concerned, he was simply stating the truth.

It can be easy at times to confuse humility with weakness or humiliation. While that doesn't seem to have been something Paul was prone to do, it is still a common way of thinking in the world today. Pride is upheld as the number one virtue, and humility is seen as a sign of insecurity and inadequacy.

How foreign this way of thinking is to the gospel! Christian humility is based on reality and was in fact the central quality of some of the greatest heroes of our faith. God wants us to understand that every talent and gift we have is a result of God's grace, and so is not something we can claim as our own doing.

We all have strengths and areas in our lives in which we are particularly gifted. When we accept this truth about ourselves—when we accept our "beauty marks" as well as our "blemishes"—we are really giving glory to God and letting his characteristics shine through us. Remember: We were created in the image and likeness of God, and so we participate in his goodness if we cooperate with him and develop the gifts he has given us. This should be a cause for rejoicing.

It should be a cause for us to let our light shine before others so they can see the Father's love in us and so be drawn closer to him (Matthew 5:14-16).

Here's a test. When someone compliments you on a job well done, do you thank the person with your lips and then thank God with your heart? Or do you try to minimize what you have done and insist on your weakness? One way is the way of humility, the other is the way of false modesty. May we nurture true humility in our hearts by giving credit to God for all he has given us!

"Father, teach me the way of humility. May I become a bold witness to your goodness and power."

2 Corinthians 11:1-15

[1] I wish you would bear with me in a little foolishness. Do bear with me! [2] I feel a divine jealousy for you, for I betrothed you to Christ to present you as a pure bride to her one husband. [3] But I am afraid that as the serpent deceived Eve by his cunning, your thoughts will be led astray from a sincere and pure devotion to Christ. [4] For if some one comes and preaches another Jesus than the one we preached, or if you receive a different spirit from the one you received, or if you accept a different gospel from the one you accepted, you submit to it readily enough. [5] I think that I am not in the least inferior to these superlative apostles. [6] Even if I am unskilled in speaking, I am not in knowledge; in every way we have made this plain to you in all things.

[7] Did I commit a sin in abasing myself so that you might be exalted, because I preached God's gospel without cost to you? [8] I robbed other

churches by accepting support from them in order to serve you. [9] And when I was with you and was in want, I did not burden any one, for my needs were supplied by the brethren who came from Macedo'nia. So I refrained and will refrain from burdening you in any way. [10] As the truth of Christ is in me, this boast of mine shall not be silenced in the regions of Acha'ia. [11] And why? Because I do not love you? God knows I do!

[12] And what I do I will continue to do, in order to undermine the claim of those who would like to claim that in their boasted mission they work on the same terms as we do. [13] For such men are false apostles, deceitful workmen, disguising themselves as apostles of Christ. [14] And no wonder, for even Satan disguises himself as an angel of light. [15] So it is not strange if his servants also disguise themselves as servants of righteousness. Their end will correspond to their deeds.

The attack on Paul's ministry forced him to defend himself against rival preachers who were contesting the gospel of Jesus Christ. These rivals had social status and polished rhetorical skills—qualities that were highly prized in the Greek world. Swayed by their flair and influence, some "sophisticated" members of the Corinthian church had become unable to make correct judgments about what these preachers were teaching. Paul's humility, poverty, and lack of oratorical ability made his message suspect in their eyes. What they failed to grasp was that Paul's simplicity verified the authenticity of his message.

These preachers, whom Paul sarcastically dubbed "super-apostles," planted seeds of doubt about Jesus' divine nature in the minds of the Corinthians (2 Corinthians 11:4-5). Although they considered Jesus a man of good spiritual qualities, they did not consider him to be the crucified and risen Son of God. Paul—anxious to protect the Corinthians from false teaching—challenged their claims, warning them against the proclamation of "another Jesus" (11:4).

Paul noted that these "super-apostles" used only human standards: "They measure themselves by one another, and compare themselves with one another" (2 Corinthians 10:12). He said they did "not show good sense" in preaching a gospel different from the one he proclaimed. And what's worse, it appears that these false teachers were expecting the Corinthians to pay them for their services—while Paul continued to refrain from making such a demand!

The heart of the Christian faith is that Jesus Christ, the incarnate Son of God, died on a cross and rose from the dead to set believers free from sin and death. "I want you to know, brothers and sisters," said Paul, "that the gospel that was proclaimed by me is not of human origin; for I did not receive it from a human source, nor was I taught it, but I received it through a revelation of Jesus Christ" (Galatians 1:11-12). Only the Spirit of Christ can convince us of this truth.

Any "gospel" that does not acknowledge Jesus Christ crucified and risen is not a true gospel. It may have a certain appeal at a basic human level. It may advocate gospel ideals such as peace, love, understanding, and freedom. But only the gospel revealed by the Holy Spirit contains the words of eternal life; it alone has the power to bring about all the blessings that any "different gospel" can only hint at.

May all who proclaim the good news proclaim the full gospel—generously and freely. And may all who hear that gospel allow the Holy Spirit to open their minds to accept it.

2 Corinthians 11:16-33

[16] I repeat, let no one think me foolish; but even if you do, accept me as a fool, so that I too may boast a little. [17] (What I am saying I say not with the Lord's authority but as a fool, in this boastful confidence; [18] since many boast of worldly things, I too will boast.) [19] For you gladly bear with fools, being wise yourselves! [20] For you bear it if a man makes slaves of you, or preys upon you, or takes advantage of you, or puts on airs, or strikes you in the face. [21] To my shame, I must say, we were too weak for that! But whatever any one dares to boast of — I am speaking as a fool — I also dare to boast of that. [22] Are they Hebrews? So am I. Are they Israelites? So am I. Are they descendants of Abraham? So am I. [23] Are they servants of Christ? I am a better one — I am talking like a madman — with far greater labors, far more imprisonments, with countless beatings, and often near death. [24] Five times I have received at the hands of the Jews the forty lashes less one. [25] Three times I have been beaten with rods; once I was stoned. Three times I have been shipwrecked; a night and a day I have been adrift at sea; [26] on frequent journeys, in danger from rivers, danger from robbers, danger from my own people, danger from Gentiles, danger in the city, danger in the wilderness, danger at sea, danger from false brethren; [27] in toil and hardship, through many a sleepless night, in hunger and thirst, often without food, in cold and exposure. [28] And, apart from other things, there is the daily pressure upon me of my anxiety for all the churches. [29] Who is weak, and I am not weak? Who is made to fall, and I am not indignant?

[30] If I must boast, I will boast of the things that show my weakness. [31] The God and Father of the Lord Jesus, he who is blessed for ever, knows that I do not lie. [32] At Damascus, the governor under King Ar'etas guarded the city of Damascus in order to seize me, [33] but I was let down in a basket through a window in the wall, and escaped his hands.

Faced with a situation in which the Corinthians were being led astray by false apostles, Paul felt the need to defend himself and try to win them back to the truth. But where we might expect Paul to talk about the numbers of people he had converted or the numbers of miracles he had performed, he gave a completely different list of qualifications. Is this the best "boasting" Paul could come up with? None of the signs of an authentic ministry that Paul used in these verses is really all that attractive. As he himself admitted, his list of hardships did nothing but reveal his own weaknesses and the ways his commitment to Christ had placed him in threatening—even seemingly foolish—circumstances.

Paul's self-defense at this point demonstrates a key characteristic of a true disciple and servant of Christ. Rather than talk about his heroic deeds, Paul went out of his way to show the kind of transformation he had experienced in Christ—and by extension, the kind of transformation that the Corinthians should be experiencing in their own lives.

That transformation began for Paul just as it begins for all of us: by being willing to set aside human standards of judging success and the desire to look good in front of other people. It's a transformation that takes place when we adopt God's criteria for success and when we obey his word, even though the results may look pitiful or foolish in human eyes. Paul knew that the "super-apostles" who were dazzling the Corinthians had not undergone this transformation. He knew they would most likely give up their so-called ministry at the first beating, the first shipwreck, or the first public humiliation.

Paul wanted to make it clear that he persevered in the face of human and spiritual opposition because he had learned how to draw strength from the Holy Spirit as he sought to adopt God's standards rather than his own. His credentials, intellect, and religious background—while all very impressive—were insufficient to give him the determination he needed to press on in his work. As he had said earlier, it was the love of Christ that compelled him (2 Corinthians 5:14).

God wants to transform us, just as he transformed Paul. He is like a refining fire that can purify us and temper us like the finest gold if we open our hearts to him. He will not force himself upon us, nor will he overtake our wills; yet, if we allow him, he will reveal his love in such a powerful way that everything else will pale in comparison. Let us open ourselves to his love and allow him to fill us with the strength to do the impossible.

"Lord, may I not rely primarily on my abilities or my strength but on your love and its transforming power in my life. Strengthen me in spirit, soul, and body, that I may be impelled by your love to pursue and respond to you alone."

2 Corinthians 12:1-10

[1] I must boast; there is nothing to be gained by it, but I will go on to visions and revelations of the Lord. [2] I know a man in Christ who fourteen years ago was caught up to the third heaven — whether in the body or out of the body I do not know, God knows. [3] And I know that this man was caught up into Paradise — whether in the body or out of the body I do not know, God knows — [4] and he heard things that cannot be told, which man may not utter. [5] On behalf of this man I will boast, but on my own behalf I will not boast, except of my weaknesses. [6] Though if I wish to boast, I shall not be a fool, for I shall be speaking the truth. But I refrain from it, so that no one may think more of me than he sees in me or hears from me. [7] And to keep me from being too elated by the abundance of revelations, a thorn was

given me in the flesh, a messenger of Satan, to harass me, to keep me from being too elated. [8] Three times I besought the Lord about this, that it should leave me; [9] but he said to me, "My grace is sufficient for you, for my power is made perfect in weakness." I will all the more gladly boast of my weaknesses, that the power of Christ may rest upon me. [10] For the sake of Christ, then, I am content with weaknesses, insults, hardships, persecutions, and calamities; for when I am weak, then I am strong.

How do you react when you're facing competition from someone? Perhaps it's a question of who is making more money, or who is a faster runner, or who is a better cook. Whatever the specific issue, when our expertise or skills are challenged, isn't it almost natural to defend ourselves with a show of strength? Isn't it an almost automatic response to prove ourselves with a demonstration of superiority?

This seems to be the kind of challenge Paul was facing from the so-called "super-apostles." These false leaders had managed to impress many of the Corinthian Christians with tales of their mystical experiences and their access to hidden wisdom from God. They had thrown down the gauntlet, and it was now up to Paul to prove himself superior—presumably on similar grounds.

But Paul did something unexpected. He didn't back down from the challenge, adopting a tone of false humility and pious selflessness. Neither did he simply shoot back with a listing of all his special experiences and revelations. Rather, he spoke somewhat guardedly about one instance—fourteen years before—when he did have a powerful experience of God, and immediately followed it with the equally guarded account of his ongoing bout with a "thorn in the flesh" (2 Corinthians 12:7). We don't know precisely what this "thorn" was, but it is clear that Paul understood it as something given him to keep him humble and reliant on God's grace and power.

So much for a boasting contest! Where Paul's opponents kept the Corinthians astounded with spectacular stories of spiritual superiority, Paul appealed to their spiritual instinct that the meek will inherit the kingdom. Just as Jesus was "crucified in weakness, but lives by the power of God" (2 Corinthians 13:4), so Paul had learned that the weaker he was, the more the Lord was able to act in and through him (12:9).

The point here is not that God delights in keeping his servants weak and helpless. This is hardly how we would characterize Paul—or the other apostles, for that matter. No, the point is that the gifts and graces God pours out upon us are not meant to give us a sense of superiority to others. They are meant to propel us into the world as servants, as ambassadors of the gospel. We do indeed hold a great treasure, but this treasure resides in us as in a humble clay jar (2 Corinthians 4:7). It is not ours to keep as we might keep precious jewelry. Rather, it is ours to give away, pointing people to the great Giver who has lavished such beautiful gifts, and not to us as the recipients of the gifts. May we all learn how to be generous receivers of God's grace, and generous givers of that grace to others. May our pride come only from the fact that God has been merciful to us and has called us into his service!

"Father, teach me to yield to you. Make me strong by the power of your Spirit. Encourage me in my difficulties and fill me with trust and confidence in you."

2 Corinthians 12:11-18

[11] I have been a fool! You forced me to it, for I ought to have been commended by you. For I was not at all inferior to these superlative apostles, even though I am nothing. [12] The signs of a true apostle were performed among you in all patience, with signs and wonders and mighty works. [13] For in what were you less favored than the rest of the churches, except that I myself did not burden you? Forgive me this wrong!

[14] Here for the third time I am ready to come to you. And I will not be a burden, for I seek not what is yours but you; for children ought not to lay up for their parents, but parents for their children. [15] I will most gladly spend and be spent for your souls. If I love you the more, am I to be loved the less? [16] But granting that I myself did not burden you, I was crafty, you say, and got the better of you by guile. [17] Did I take advantage of you through any of those whom I sent to you? [18] I urged Titus to go, and sent the brother with him. Did Titus take advantage of you? Did we not act in the same spirit? Did we not take the same steps?

Paul saw himself as a spiritual father to the Corinthian church, and like a father who spends himself for his children, he had poured himself out for the members of this church (1 Corinthians 4:15). Now, in a dramatic outburst of emotion, he expresses his feelings to them—how much he loved them; how much he longed for their affection; and how deeply hurt he was by their suspicions and accusations.

As was his usual practice, Paul preached the gospel among the Corinthians without accepting any financial support from them. Instead, he earned his keep by working as a tentmaker (Acts 18:1-3). His intentions were completely honorable—he didn't want to be a burden to anyone—but this poor fellow just couldn't win for losing! In what can only be called classic irony, it seems that Paul's unwillingness to accept money made the Corinthians feel that he was questioning *their* commitment to *him*. If he really loved them, they reasoned, he would accept their money, just as his opponents had been quick to receive support from them.

But Paul wasn't interested in their money; he wanted their love. Sore of heart, he wrote: "I seek not what is yours but you. . . . I will most gladly spend and be spent for your souls" (2 Corinthians 12:14,15). Why, Paul asked, should the free gift of his love make the Corinthians consider him undeserving of their own love in return?

These verses paint a moving picture of Paul as a pastor with a very human heart. This is something we can easily overlook, even when we look at our own pastors, bishops, and other church leaders. Today, countless men and women all over the world are pouring out their lives for the sake of the people of God. From missionaries in far-off lands to religious sisters in the inner cities, they have chosen to give up the comforts of the world and to risk their lives to bring the love and grace of Christ to as many as possible. Let's pray today for them. Let's ask God to fill them with his comfort and encouragement.

"Heavenly Father, bless and strengthen all those who spend themselves so generously on your church. You alone know the depths of their love for those you have entrusted to their care. You alone know the cost of the sacrifices they make on behalf of those you have called them to serve. Father, be their comfort and give them joy in their labors."

2 Corinthians 12:19-21

[19] Have you been thinking all along that we have been defending ourselves before you? It is in the sight of God that we have been speaking in Christ, and all for your upbuilding, beloved. [20] For I fear that perhaps I may come and find you not what I wish, and that you may find me not what you wish; that perhaps there may be quarreling, jealousy, anger, selfishness, slander, gossip, conceit, and disorder. [21] I fear that when I come again my God may humble me before you, and I may have to mourn over many of those who sinned before and have not repented of the impurity, immorality, and licentiousness which they have practiced.

Just thinking about seeing a loved one again after a long separation or absence makes your heart beat faster, doesn't it? Perhaps your son or daughter moved to a distant state after marrying several years ago, and now you are planning your first visit together since then. Maybe there's a friend you haven't seen since high school days, and soon you'll meet at a class reunion. Your excitement grows day by day as you happily look forward to the encounter. Yet, possibly there's a touch of apprehension mixed in with your joy and sense of anticipation: "Has my daughter matured into the woman I've envisioned from her letters and phone calls?" "I've changed so much since our graduation. What will Joe think of me after all these years?" Paul had similar apprehensions as he wrote to the Corinthians about his impending visit: "I fear that perhaps I may come and find you not what I wish, and that you may find me not what you wish" (2 Corinthians 12:20).

Paul worried that the Corinthians were caught up again in the quarreling, jealousies, slanderous speech, immoral behavior, and other vices that he had previously encountered among them (2 Corinthians 12:20-21). While he loved them and longed to see them, he feared that they had strayed from the gospel he had taught them and its implications for the way they treated one another. Would he find members of the church in Corinth divided among themselves? Would they be critical of him again? Had some fallen back into their former pagan moral laxity? If so, he would have to act firmly with them—and thus possibly increase the tension between himself and them again.

Paul didn't like defending himself to the Corinthians or correcting their failings, but he was willing to take a strong stand when the spiritual welfare of the community was at stake: "It is in the sight of God that we have been speaking in Christ, and all for your upbuilding, beloved" (2 Corinthians 12:19).

If Paul were to visit us today, would he find us "as he wished"—manifesting the gospel and the life of God in us through loving relationships with our brothers and sisters in Christ? Or would he find that our sins, like those of the Corinthians, are damaging the bonds that knit us together in the body of Christ—bonds of love, humility, and service to one another? Let's prayerfully examine our hearts and ask the Holy Spirit to help us renew our efforts to live a life in keeping with Christ who is present in us.

2 Corinthians 13:1-10

[1] This is the third time I am coming to you. Any charge must be sustained by the evidence of two or three witnesses. [2] I warned those who sinned before and all the others, and I warn them now while absent, as I did when present on my second visit, that if I come again I will not spare them — [3] since you desire proof that Christ is speaking in me. He is not weak in dealing with you, but is powerful in you. [4] For he was crucified in weakness, but lives by the power of God. For we are weak in him, but in dealing with you we shall live with him by the power of God.

[5] Examine yourselves, to see whether you are holding to your faith. Test yourselves. Do you not realize that Jesus Christ is in you? — unless indeed you fail to meet the test! [6] I hope you will find out that we have not failed. [7] But we pray God that you may not do wrong — not that we may appear to have met the test, but that you may do what is right, though we may seem to have failed. [8] For we cannot do anything against the truth, but only for the truth. [9] For we are glad when we are weak and you are strong. What we pray for is your improvement. [10] I write this while I am away from you, in order that when I come I may not have to be severe in my use of the authority which the Lord has given me for building up and not for tearing down.

As Paul brought this difficult letter to a close, his thoughts returned to two themes he often wrote about to the churches throughout Asia Minor. First, he reminded the Corinthians that Christ, though crucified in weakness, lives by the power of God (2 Corinthians 13:4). This was the same paradox he had eloquently proclaimed at the beginning of First Corinthians: "The word of the cross is folly to those who are perishing, but to us who are being saved it is the power of God" (1 Corinthians 1:18).

In his death Jesus appeared to be weak. However, by rising from the dead he manifested his divine power, for "the foolishness of God is wiser than men, and the weakness of God is stronger than men" (1 Corinthians 1:25). Now Paul, who appeared to be weak in the eyes of the trouble-ridden and rebellious Corinthians, applied this theme to himself when he reminded them of his God-given authority as an apostle—"Christ is speaking in me" (2 Corinthians 13:3)—to correct and admonish them (13:10). Though weak himself, in dealing with the Corinthians Paul would exercise the power of God (13:4).

Paul then coupled this paradox with another of his great themes, his teaching that every Christian has indeed been crucified with Christ. Paul told the Christians in Rome that through baptism, we are dead to sin and alive to Christ (Romans 6:3-11). Likewise, he told the Galatians, "I have been crucified with Christ; it is no longer I who live but Christ who lives in me" (Galatians 2:20). Now Paul urges the Corinthians to examine both their hearts and their actions to see if they were really living in this reality: "Do you not realize that Jesus Christ is in you?" (2 Corinthians 13:5).

Let's take our cue from Paul's advice to the Corinthians. A daily examination of conscience or periodic review of our life can help us know ourselves better. Asking the Holy Spirit to help us look at our lives objectively can help show us where we have gained or lost ground in our Christian life. Like taking a compass reading, such an examination can help us find our bearings again—whether to keep on track, to chart a new path to God, or to make any corrections needed in our course.

As we come to the end of this letter, let's reaffirm, along with St. Paul and the ancient Corinthians, that we have indeed died to sin and that Christ really does live in us. Let's take hold of the new life Jesus has poured out upon us. And let's never tire of examining ourselves, so that we can become more and more like Jesus, whose strength can enable us to do far more than we can ever ask or imagine.

"Thank you, Lord Jesus, that you were crucified in weakness and raised in power for my sake. Fill me with your power so that your image shines through my weakness."

2 Corinthians 13:11-14

[11] Finally, brethren, farewell. Mend your ways, heed my appeal, agree with one another, live in peace, and the God of love and peace will be with you. [12] Greet one another with a holy kiss. [13] All the saints greet you.

[14] The grace of the Lord Jesus Christ and the love of God and the fellowship of the Holy Spirit be with you all.

Lord Jesus, we give honor and praise and glory to your holy name! Through you, we have been baptized into the very life of the Trinity. The grace of the Lord Jesus Christ and the love of God and the fellowship of the Holy Spirit are now ours. We praise you for your generosity and love!

Jesus, how marvelous is your grace! You have freely given us something that we never could have obtained on our own: You have delivered us from death! Thank you for sweeping away our sins like dust. Thank you for redeeming us. Thank you for turning our mourning into dancing. You have raised us up to be with you. You have withheld no good thing from us. Through your blood, you have made us blameless and righteous in the sight of God the Father.

Gracious Father! Before we were born, you knew and loved each and every one of us. You created us to know and receive your overflowing love. You promised that you would never forget us, and you haven't. You have engraved us on the palm of your hand. Even before we knew you, while we were still lost in sin, you showed your love by sending your Son to die in our place, so that we might inherit eternal life. We praise you for your everlasting love and compassion—love that never condemns us when we fail you, but always forgives, always draws us back, always comforts and heals.

Blessed Holy Spirit, our Comforter, how amazing that we should have fellowship with you! All praise and glory to you who dwell in us, giving us unhindered access to the throne of God. You lead and guide us in all truth. You speak the words of the Father to our hearts. Thank you, Holy Spirit, for revealing Jesus to us, for opening our hearts and minds to know him personally. Thank you for teaching us his ways and reminding us of his words. Day after day, you conform us to his image, gently but persistently, so that more and more we resemble the One for whom we were created. Thank you for such faithfulness!

"Blessed Trinity, may we praise you all our days for the awesome grace of being allowed to share in your life!"